PLAN A
PROFITABLE
BOOK
LAUNCH

PLAN A PROFITABLE BOOK LAUNCH

Copyright © 2021 by Mandi Lynn

For information contact :

Bethany Atazadeh : http://www.bethanyatazadeh.com

Mandi Lynn : mandi@stoneridgebooks.com

Cover design by Stone Ridge Books

Formatting by Bethany Atazadeh

ISBN : 978-1-953388-04-9

First Edition: October 2021

10 9 8 7 6 5 4 3 2 1

MARKETING FOR AUTHORS

PLAN A PROFITABLE BOOK LAUNCH

Create a Successful Book Release Strategy with Publishing Timelines, Pre-Order Campaigns, Getting Reviews, & More!

MANDI LYNN
WITH BETHANY ATAZADEH

Introduction

WELCOME TO BOOK five in the Marketing for Authors series! In this book, we're going to be talking about all the things you need to juggle when it comes to marketing a new book leading up to release day. There's a *lot* to cover when it comes to book launches, and in this book, we're going to take a deep dive into planning your book release, specifically your *marketing process* for that release. It's impossible to talk about marketing without also talking about the publishing process, but please know this is not a book about how to publish a novel. Instead, we'll be talking about the points where marketing and publishing intersect, as well as some logistics to get you started. The goal of this book is to help you plan a profitable book release to maximize on the most exciting day of your book's lifetime.

As you work through the chapters of this book, you'll discover some of the endless ways you can choose to market your book launch. You'll create a book publishing and marketing timeline, and use that timeline to streamline your work process leading up to release.

Throughout the book you'll be learning a handful of marketing techniques that you can choose to do when you're releasing your book. This includes starting a pre-order campaign, sending out advanced reader copies, having a street team, and so much more. We'll talk about how to take full advantage of your book cover, and how to use it as a marketing tool to encourage sales long before release day. Other marketing techniques that will be covered include planning a virtual book tour, creating a book trailer, and hosting book signing events. All these tools are effective for different reasons, and we'll go through the pros and cons of each, and some helpful tips so you can properly implement these strategies.

First and foremost, you should know that the marketing techniques I talk about in this book are things that I have done and tried myself. That does not mean these are your only options, so feel free to explore other areas to research different marketing methods. You'll also hear from my co-author, Bethany Atazadeh, at the end of every chapter. You may notice that we have different experiences when it comes to different things, as is typical in the publishing world. Most of the time you have to try different marketing techniques yourself to see what works for you.

Second, book launches work very differently depending on different genres. What Bethany and I do to promote the Marketing for Authors series is very different from what we do when we release one of our fiction books. As you read, I will try to give you as many examples of marketing options as possible to get your creative juices flowing. Then you can decide for yourself what will work for your book. When it comes to choosing how to market your book, always think about the best way to reach your *ideal reader,* a topic discussed in detail in book three of the Marketing for Authors series, *Book Sales That Multiply.*

Which brings me to my third point: a lot of what is talked about in this book touches on things we've covered in books one through four. Please read the other books in this series before reading this book, since this is the point where everything you've learned comes together. The book launch process can be extremely overwhelming, but it can also be a lot of fun. Take your time when planning, and make your story heard.

Finally, you can do all the best marketing in the world, but if your book isn't good quality, marketing means nothing. So many authors, myself included, get so excited to publish their book, that they skim across very important parts of the book creation process. Do not let yourself get so distracted by the fun of a book release that you rush the editing process. Your book—those words you've written and labored over for months, maybe even years—is the most important part of this entire process. And now that your book is ready to be published, it's time to start marketing!

Things You've Already Learned

Throughout this book, I'll be building on the tools and techniques you've already learned and hopefully, have put into action!

Book one in this series, *How Your Book Sells Itself*, is all about setting your book up for success. Like I mentioned, your book is the most important part in this process. We identified the ten elements that help sell your book:

1. The Story
2. Genre
3. Cover
4. Title
5. Book Blurb
6. Taglines
7. Formatting
8. Editing
9. Keywords
10. Categories

Creating the book is only half the task. As you read through this book, you'll quickly learn that planning a release, and releasing the book in a timely manner is all about multitasking and overlapping tasks. You may be doing line and copy editing while you're also doing a cover reveal and taking pre-orders. If you're releasing your first book, it's usually best to give yourself more time than you think necessary to finish tasks. As you publish more books, you'll get a better understanding of how long it takes *you* to edit a book and to complete each step in the process. As you grow more experienced, you can streamline the process more and take less time for each task, but if this is your first book, be generous with the deadlines you give yourself.

In book two in the series, *Grow Your Author Platform*, we help you implement tips to develop your author platform as soon as possible. All too often I hear from authors who say, "How do I market a book if I don't have a platform?" My answer will always be, "Go make yourself a platform so you can talk about your book." Instead of settling with the fact that you don't have a large platform, learn how to make it grow. Or how to make your small platform full of loyal followers willing to buy your book. There are many things you can start doing today to get your author platform off to a healthy start, such as:

- Create an author website.
- Build an email list.
- Learn the benefits of content marketing and how search engine optimization makes you show up to new readers. Content marketing can include, but is not limited to, YouTube, Pinterest, and blogs.

Book three in the series, *Book Sales That Multiply*, covers everything you need to know to take your sales and make them grow exponentially. The most important thing you'll learn is the significance of your ideal reader and how to target them. Targeting your ideal reader is all about focusing your efforts to the person who is most likely to enjoy reading and leave a glowing five-star review of your book. Besides learning about how to find your ideal reader, in this book you also learned about:

- Free versus paid marketing.
- Creating graphics and sales copy.
- Newsletter swaps and features.
- eBook promotion sites.
- Goodreads giveaways.
- Facebook ads.
- Amazon ads

Then we have book four in this series, *Secrets to Selling Books on Social Media*. In this book you covered everything about marketing your book on social media. It's not just about making the most aesthetically pleasing post. Rather, this book is about the technical side behind writing copy for your social media posts and how to gain trust with your audience so they'll eventually buy your book. Some of the social media strategies covered in this book include:

- The entrepreneur versus influencer mindset.
- The know, like, and trust principle.
- Multiple sales formulas.
- Posting categories.
- Post templates.
- Content calendars.

Which leads to book five, *Plan a Profitable Book Launch*. As already mentioned, we'll be covering some of the most common marketing techniques used by indie authors to plan a book release. My hope is that by the time you finish reading this book, you'll have an idea of what strategies you'll want to implement for your release. While there's no "one way" to publish a book, my hope is that by reading this book and learning from successes and failures that Bethany and I have experienced, you'll be able to create your book release strategy with more confidence.

Chapter 1: One Million & Two Things To Do

THE BEAUTY OF self-publishing is that you get to decide everything! The worst part of self-publishing is also that you have to decide everything. And by decide, I also mean you have to do everything yourself. In this chapter we're going to list out some of the many things that you'll have to decide, from the publishing side of things, like ISBN's; to the marketing side of things, like how you're going to get reviews for your book.

You can hire people to help you, like cover designers and editors, but when it comes to marketing, you'll usually have the best results if you do it yourself. Yes, I know it's tempting to hire a digital assistant or someone else for a couple hundred dollars to market your book for you. It may feel like, "Well, if I hire a pro to market my book, that's guaranteed sales, right?" Nope!

The person who knows your book best is *you*. Therefore, you are the best person for the job when it comes to marketing. And let's face the facts: marketing is all about experimenting. There are books upon books on marketing, but here's what they don't tell you: the only way to find the type of marketing that will work best for you is to experiment. If there's no clear way of what's right or wrong, why hire someone else when you can do it yourself? Yes, it will take time, but trust me when I say it's more worth spending your time, than it is your money.

For example: I wanted to create an ad for *The Book Launch Planner*, which is a planner designed to help authors organize themselves during the publishing process. The planner had been selling really well by itself, so I wanted to double sales by investing in Instagram ads. In order to do that, I had to experiment with four different rounds of sales copy, six different images and graphics, and three different landing pages. Experimenting with that many logistics to get the right outcome can take weeks, sometimes months. And even after all of that, you may sometimes say to yourself, "Well, that was a waste of time."

You often don't know what marketing techniques do or don't work until you test them.

It's All About the Return on Investment

One thing you'll learn as you work through this book is that not all types of marketing are free. If they are free, they tend to take up a lot of time. Any type of marketing will cost you either money, time, or both. This book will give you a lot of options to market, and you won't be able to do it all. As you read, you'll have to make decisions about what strategies you want to try. Always keep ROI (Return On Investment) in mind. If you've read the previous books in the series, you've heard me talk about ROI before.

ROI is defined as a metric used to measure the profitability of an investment. In the publishing world it might be hard, or sometimes impossible, to come up with an actual number for ROI. However, you should be able to make a rough estimate of whether or not a marketing technique is worth your time or money. Whenever you do any marketing tactic, always be sure to ask yourself what results you're looking for that will make your time or money worth it.

For example, let's say you're looking to get book reviews so you plan on reaching out to twenty book bloggers. How many book bloggers would you say *need* to review your book to be worth your time? If you feel it's only worth your time if they all read and review your book, then reaching out to reviewers won't be worth your time because that very rarely—if ever—happens. If you're okay with even just five of the bloggers reviewing your book, then it should be worth your time!

It can be hard to predict what will and won't be worth your time, but as long as you keep in mind your expectations and keep your goals realistic, you

PLAN A PROFITABLE BOOK LAUNCH should be able to differentiate what marketing techniques will be a good fit for you.

Develop Your To-Do List

One of the first things you'll want to do when you're planning your book launch is to create your to-do list. Start off by writing down every marketing idea that pops into your head, as well as everything you need to do to get the book published. Here's a start...

Publishing To-Do's:

- Developmental edits
- Line and copy edits
- Proofreading
- Formatting
- Cover design
- Book blurb
- Book title
- Book keyword and genre research

This is only a tiny sample of to-do's you'll come across when publishing. Since this is a book on marketing, rather than publishing, please make sure to check out the resources section of this book to learn more about the publishing process.

Marketing To-Do's:

- Street team
- Blog/Instagram tour
- Advanced Reader Copies, often called ARCs (and how to distribute them)
- Cover reveal
- Newsletter promo sites (BookBub being the biggest example)
- Book trailer
- Paid advertising (Instagram, Facebook, Amazon, etc.)
- Release day event(s)
- Giveaways

You can very quickly create a long list of marketing ideas, and it's up to you to narrow the list down to something that is manageable for your schedule. One of the easiest ways to narrow down your marketing to-do list is to highlight the tasks you're the most familiar and comfortable with doing.

If you want to do a book trailer just because it sounds cool, but you have no idea how to even start that process, it might be beneficial to remove that from your to-do list—at least for now.

Decision fatigue is something you'll become very familiar with over the course of your publishing career. You can publish fifty books and still release every single book differently. As you read, you'll see there's no one way to publish a book.

To prevent decision fatigue for myself, I have a group of author friends that I go to when I need to bounce ideas off of them. When I'm torn between two different options, I present them to these friends and see what they think.

Not everyone will have a back pocket of friends who are authors, but most people have at least one person in their life who's rooting them on in the publishing process. Whether that person is your spouse, parent, or friend, go to them when you're feeling decision fatigue and you need a fresh perspective on the situation.

Besides publishing and marketing, there are also some logistical things you'll need to decide.

Logistical To-Do's:

- What formats will your book be in? (paperback, eBook, hardcover, audiobook)

- Where will you distribute your print book? (Kindle Direct Publishing, IngramSpark, Barnes & Noble Press, or other options)

- Where will you distribute your eBook? (Draft2Digital, Smashwords, Kindle Direct Publishing, IngramSpark, or other options)

To answer some of these questions you'll end up asking yourself additional questions. Some of them are simple, like deciding whether or not you want to physically hold your book in your hands. However, other logistics get a little more complicated. To make some of these decisions, it's best to research all the pro's and con's for each option.

What Formats Will Your Book Be In?

- **eBook** – Indie authors often make the most overall royalties from eBook sales since there's less risk for a new reader to buy an eBook for a few dollars versus a paperback for five times that cost. However, for those who dream of holding their book in their hands one day, having only an eBook edition of their book can feel a little lackluster.

- **Paperback** - Most indie authors will choose to do a paperback as well as an eBook edition of their book because this offers the best of both worlds. While the cost of printing a paperback will cut into your royalty rate, print on demand companies keep the cost of printing reasonable, leaving authors room for profit.

- **Hardcover** - For those who love and adore hardcover editions of books, it can feel like a must to do a hardcover edition of their book. The downside is that hardcover sales will almost always make you the least amount of money. Most print on demand companies print hardcovers at a much higher cost, which means you'll have to charge more for your book. Not only will you get fewer sales because it's more expensive to print, but you will also make less royalties per sale.

- **Audiobook** - What didn't used to be an option

for indie authors is now becoming more and more popular. There are multiple companies that authors can use to work with narrators to record an audiobook, such as ACX or Findaway Voices. Authors can either split royalties with the narrator, or pay a fixed price for the creation of the audiobook. Most indie authors choose not to go the audiobook route because of how expensive it can be, but as audiobooks become more and more popular, you can see indie authors experiment with it more.

Where Will You Distribute Your Print Book?

There are countless ways to print your book, but in this case we'll just mention the three most popular options. I'll go over some of the biggest pro's and con's, but please do further research before making final decisions for your book.

- **Kindle Direct Publishing** - Probably the most popular print on demand company is Kindle Direct Publishing (KDP). Owned by Amazon, they often have extremely helpful customer service, quality paperbacks, and a platform that is user-friendly. The biggest downside of KDP (at the time of writing this) is the inability to do pre-orders for physical books. While they do offer expanded distribution, retailers do not have the option to return the book if it doesn't sell. The biggest downside most authors face with KDP is that when you order a copy of your book before publication day, a large "Not for Resale" ribbon is printed across the cover. While this may not be a deal breaker for you, it can make marketing difficult when the only print copy you have of your book has a portion of the cover obscured.

- **IngramSpark** - IngramSpark offers wide distribution (meaning, your book will be sold on multiple vendors outside of just Amazon) with the options for retailers to return unsold books. They offer eBook, hardcover, and paperback formats, as well as provide a pre-order option for all three. However, because it is such a large and professional scale platform, there are a few cons that first-time authors should be aware of. Some of these include publishing fees (fees for adding new books and updating files), slightly higher printing costs, customer service that's available only through email, longer timeframes for files to update, and a platform that's not always the most user-friendly. IngramSpark, while a valuable tool, may not be the best option for beginners because the platform is not forgiving if you make mistakes. If you're considering IngramSpark, I highly suggest visiting the resource section of this book for more information.

- **Barnes and Noble Press** - Barnes and Noble Press is newer to the print on demand world, but it's becoming a great option for those that want the benefits of IngramSpark without the fear of using the platform incorrectly. A little-known fact is that Barnes and Noble Press uses the same printer as IngramSpark, so you get the same quality out of your paperbacks and hardcovers, but instead you're working with Barnes and Noble Press. In a lot of ways, it's just like working with IngramSpark in terms of print quality, but you have Barnes and Noble Press acting as the middleman in terms of customer service. The main pro is that you don't need to pay any uploading fees. However the distribution will be solely through Barnes & Noble online stores, not other retailers.

Where Will You Distribute Your eBook?

- **Draft2Digital** - Draft2Digital is a one-stop shop for uploading your eBook. They work with most eBook retailers and have just recently begun to distribute print books as well! Their options for print books are brand new, so while I can't say anything on that, I can say their dashboard for uploading eBooks is easy to use. In fact, you can also use Draft2Digital to format your book. They offer many tools for authors including universal book links, author pages, and more to help you promote your books.

- **Smashwords** - Smashwords is very similar to Draft2Digital in the sense that it will also get you listed on most major eBook retailers. However, at this time their platform is much older and less user-friendly. Smashwords also doesn't offer any other services besides uploading your book, so you'll need to make sure your book is already formatted correctly for eBook.

- **Kindle Direct Publishing** - KDP only offers distribution for Kindle, which can sound like a downside if you want wide distribution to all eBook retailers for your eBook. However being only on Kindle can have its benefits. When your book is only on Kindle, you can enroll in the Kindle Unlimited program, which allows you to host sales and be paid by pages read, rather than by books sold. The program is a bit more complicated than that, so please check out the resources section of this book for more information.

- **IngramSpark** - I personally have never used IngramSpark's eBook distribution. While they do offer wide distribution, IngramSpark is the only company that requires a fee of $25-$50 whenever you upload a book to be published or update files. For that reason, most authors shy away from using IngramSpark for eBooks.

This is only a sample of some of the things you'll need to consider when publishing. While I can't cover all the logistics of self-publishing in this book, I highly recommend doing more research. A great way to start would be by checking out the resources section of this book!

BONUS TIP FROM BETHANY:

Creating a to-do list for your book release is both incredibly overwhelming and one of my favorite parts of the job, all at the same time! It's obviously a pretty huge undertaking, no matter how you look at it. Even after publishing over ten books, I still experience the same overwhelm when I look at the big picture. So don't feel bad if you need to approach it a little bit at a time.

The way Mandi broke down the publishing to-do list into three sections can also be a good way for you to get started. First, figure out the publishing-specific list. Once you feel confident about those decisions, it could actually make some of your marketing and logistical decisions easier as well!

Second, get a sense of what you might want to do for your marketing strategy—and don't worry, it's not set in stone! You can always change and adapt your plans leading up to your release if you find that there's too much to do, or that you want to add something new.

The most important thing to note is that there's no "right" way to publish. So don't feel like you have to do every single item on this checklist, because they're *not* all requirements. But almost all of these decisions have multiple good options. The best choice for you will depend on *you* and *your* book, which includes a million other things such as your personal skill set, comfort level, and experience, plus your genre, your target readers, where they hang out online, and so much more. This is why, as you begin to read on and research the different items on this list more in-depth, if you discover someone telling you, "This is the only way to successfully release a book," I can almost guarantee they're wrong.

We are *not* going to share with you the "only" way. We are going to break down dozens of different choices and strategies that you'll run into on your publishing journey, along with our honest opinions of all of them. What we share within these pages is *just* a starting place, where we help you skip a few painful learning curves. We'll share our own publishing experiences (and mistakes) so you don't have to learn the hard way and can instead successfully launch your book with ease and confidence.

Chapter 2: Start Marketing Yesterday

ONE OF THE most common questions I get from authors is, "When should I start marketing my book?" The answer is yesterday. The sooner you start marketing, the better. In this chapter, we'll be talking about simple, easy, and effective ways you can start marketing your book before it's time to reveal the cover, the title, or any of those *big* book marketing moments.

Technically speaking, marketing your book starts the second you tell someone about it, even if you haven't finished the first draft of the book. For example, when I wrote my newest novel, *Meet Me at the Summit*, I made it a point to talk about every step of the process on my YouTube channel. I did this because it was fun to document, it kept me accountable during the writing process, and also because it was a way for me to slowly start marketing the book long before it was published. If I talk about the story and get my fans excited for it, now they're more likely to want to pre-order it when the time comes.

This would be considered soft marketing, where you're not saying, "Buy my book!" You're just letting people know you're creating a book.

I know what you're thinking: "What if something changes?" Well, that's the beauty of it. By being open about my journey as I write a book, I'm giving readers behind the scenes access to how it was created. This means when they buy the book and finally read it, they realize, "Oh, I remember how the author mentioned struggling to write this scene." It doesn't lessen the reader's experience. If anything, it makes the reader appreciate the story more to see how it has evolved.

You don't have to talk about the plot of your

book to market your book. I posted writing vlogs on my YouTube channel about *Meet Me at the Summit* for about two months before I ever mentioned the premise of the book. To market your book, sometimes all you have to say is, "Hey, I'm writing a book." People who are interested in you and the stories you tell will follow along if you build a genuine relationship with them. So be open and honest about your struggles of writing the book and share all the fun details of the story between the struggles. And of course, you don't have to share on YouTube. Share wherever your platform is.

The Shift From Soft Marketing to Hard Marketing

During the soft marketing phase, you're just talking about creating the book. Shifting into hard marketing means you're getting ready to release the book and you want people to buy it. For me, I feel like the moment when the official marketing kicks in is when I reveal the title of the book. Some people will reveal the title right away, but for me, I like to save it until I'm ready to kick marketing into full gear.

When I wrote the first draft of *Meet Me at the Summit*, I could count on one hand how many people knew the final title of the book. To everyone else who follows me on social media, the book was referred to as Project Road Trip, which is the working title I used when I started drafting during National Novel Writing Month. Posting on social media saying, "Hey, I'm working on Project Road Trip today!" is a form of soft marketing.

I purposefully withheld the title because I was saving it for a reveal in the last week of April, which is when the hard marketing for the book officially began.

After I reveal the title, a week later I make posts on social media saying that I'm revealing the cover soon and that you can sign up to be a part of the cover reveal (we'll talk more about cover reveals later). The next week I reveal the release date, and then two weeks after that I reveal the cover of the book. A couple weeks after that, I start posting more consistently about the book with the purpose of getting more pre-order sales. This type of marketing when you're directing your followers to do something—like sign up for a cover reveal or pre-order a book—is *hard* marketing. For the sake of building a genuine relationship with your followers, it's always best to start with soft marketing before you shift into hard marketing. Even then, when you make the shift into hard marketing, you still want to keep doing the soft marketing: aka, talking about your book without asking your followers to buy it.

Whenever I make the shift from soft marketing to hard marketing, my goal is to space out reveals over the course of a few weeks so I have as many excuses to talk about my book as possible. I don't want to reveal everything in one day, because then what am I going to talk about next week? And if you reveal too many things at once, some things you reveal may not get the attention they deserve.

When I reveal my title, I like to use a graphic of the text. If possible, use the exact font that is used for your cover. If you're lucky, your font is eye-catching and even that tiny reveal of the font, will make people that much more excited for the final cover.

When you reveal the title, it's also a good time to add your book to Goodreads. Instead of uploading the cover of the book, you can keep the placeholder cover that Goodreads provides, or upload a stand-in cover, which will be the graphic you created using the font on the cover. Please note, if you upload a stand-in cover to Goodreads, you'll need a Goodreads Librarian to upload the final cover for you. You can access help from a Goodreads Librarian by making a post in their Goodreads group, which will be linked in the resources section of this book.

Whether you create a graphic of the title for Goodreads, or just to post on social media, make it simple. I highly recommend a simple white background with black text. The reason I say to do this is because if you do anything fancier, people will assume it's the cover. I've seen this happen all the time. You don't want people to assume you've revealed the cover of your book, because you don't want them to judge a book by what they think is its cover. A plain black and white graphic makes it clear that the only thing you're revealing is the title.

BONUS TIP FROM BETHANY:

Still trying to figure out how to get started? Soft marketing, where you begin talking about your product before it's ready to buy, can be a little harder to nail down than hard marketing (aka your stereotypical "buy my book" post with a link). But you might be surprised by how easy it is, how similar it is to hard marketing, and how smooth the transition can be between the two.

Like Mandi said, soft marketing, at its core, is simply talking about your work and getting your future readers excited about it. Here are some quick examples of soft marketing your book:

- Behind the scenes of your writing day.
- Go into detail about a specific character, the world, or plot.
- Talk about a specific moment in the book.
- Mention your favorite themes of the story.
- Share how you came up with the story.
- Quote a favorite line or two of dialogue from a character.
- Share the first line of the book.

When you transition into hard marketing, the only real difference should be that you have *more* to share, such as a cover, the book description, and a link to buy!

Many people think that hard marketing is transitioning into *just* the call to action (aka "here's the link to the book, go buy it!"), but that's not the case at all.

The core goal between soft and hard marketing doesn't actually change. No matter what, your marketing goal is to introduce your story to potential new readers, get them excited and interested in it, and then give them the information on where/how they can buy it. Soft marketing and hard marketing should both hit those first two steps, but soft marketing often has to stop there because you don't have the purchasing information quite yet.

If you approach marketing this way, you'll find that the transition from soft to hard marketing is seamless, and that they're both equally effective and enjoyable—not only for you, but for your readers too!

Chapter 3: Use Your Book's Pitch to Market

YOU CAN START marketing before telling anyone what the book is about. But what do you do when you need to be able to pitch your book to a friend, family member or stranger?

Eventually the time will come where you need to start telling people the premise of the story, and one of the best things you can do as an author is to already have a pitch ready to go. There's nothing worse than when someone asks what your book is about, and you panic with no clue what to say. Having a pitch ready, not only prevents panic, but gives you confidence to start selling your book! The more confident you are when pitching your book, the more interested readers will be.

In *The Book Launch Planner*, there's a page that gives you prompts to learn different ways to pitch your book to readers. The goal is to create multiple one-sentence pitches that describe your book. Use some of the prompts below to come up with different ways to describe your book.

Write a Pitch Using Your Book's...

- **Selling Point** - Your book's selling point is usually the big picture idea of the story. For those familiar with the *Save the Cat* technique of outlining, it's the promise of the premise. For *Meet Me at the Summit*, the selling point is the fact that Marly is going on a cross-country road trip to find herself after wallowing in her grief for nine months.

- **Genre** - Pitching your book using your genre is just pointing out what makes the book fit nicely into its category. If your book is a fantasy novel, what are the fantasy elements that readers will love?

- **Comparative Titles** - Comp (or comparative) titles are a great tool for authors to use to convey what their book is like based on books that readers are already familiar with. For example, I'm sure we're all familiar with publishers printing: "For fans of *Twilight*" on book covers. That's a way of pitching a book based on comp titles. Another example I've seen is *The Selection* by Kiera Cass pitched as "*The Hunger Games* meets *The Bachelor* in a new teen book series." Even though *The Bachelor* is a TV show, not a book, it gets the point across of what the story will be about based on mainstream media.

- **Opening Scene** - For this pitch you only want to focus on the opening scene of your book. What's intriguing about the first chapter that will hook someone in?

These prompts are just starting places to learn how to pitch your book. I recommend you try other ways of pitching your book as well. One of the benefits of this exercise is that by learning to get creative with short pitches, you'll be able to come up with your book's blurb.

The Dreaded Blurb

Your book blurb is the short description of your book that is on the back of your cover and on online retailers. It's the thing that, after a reader sees a stunning cover, convinces them, "Yes, I need this book." In the process of writing your blurb, you'll probably go through many revisions, questioning every piece of it, until it's finalized.

Eventually the time will come that you will need to reveal your book blurb. You can reveal it whenever you want, but for myself, I tend to wait until the book is up for pre-order. The main reason for this is that I usually don't get around to revealing the blurb until the pre-order for the book is online and the cover is revealed. I also often wait to reveal until the pre-order is available because I like to tease information as much as possible leading up to the pre-order, revealing only small bits of information at a time.

Other authors choose to reveal their book's blurb much sooner. There's no set rules for when to reveal, and there's also no "typical" time when authors reveal their blurbs. While you may be like me and wait until the very last moment to reveal your final blurb, at the very least you'll need an elevator pitch to describe your book to your followers to keep them interested.

The Magic of the Elevator Pitch

Now that you've got a basic idea of pitching your book, it's time to perfect that into an elevator pitch.

Your elevator pitch can be one of the best things you can have in your back pocket. This is a great way to pitch your book to your audience until you're ready to reveal the full description or blurb for your book. It's called an elevator pitch because the theory is that you should be able to hook someone into reading your book in the time it takes to ride an elevator. I like to set myself a limit of two sentences. I want you to not only write an elevator pitch for your book, but to memorize it. Heck, put it in the notes section of your phone so whenever someone on social media asks what your book is about, you can copy and paste it.

Here are some examples of elevator pitches for my books:

- *Essence* – After becoming an Essence—something that exists spiritually, not physically—Emma is forced to watch over her family as they deal with her supposed death.

- *I am Mercy* – The prequel to *Essence*. In 14th century France, Aida is being accused of witchcraft during the Black Plague. Outcast by her family, she tries to save the ones she loves from the plague and unlocks a dark magic and immortality.

- *She's Not Here* – After losing her father to Alzheimer's, Willow is terrified of succumbing to the disease herself and searches for a cure no matter the cost, even if it means taking an innocent life.

- *Meet Me At the Summit* – After losing both parents in a car accident, Marley is forced to face her grief and guilt when friends and family encourage her to go on a cross-country road trip to find herself and learn to live again.

One way I practice my pitches is when I'm at book signings and people ask what each book is about. I only have a handful of seconds to convince someone whether or not to buy the book. The more I pitch a book, the more I can tell whether or not the pitch works. If the same pitch continually results in book sales, I know to keep using that pitch.

Before the book is released, you might not have this exact opportunity of pitching your book to strangers at a book signing. However, you can re-create the situation by pitching your book to friends and family. Try to describe your book in one sentence. If they show interest in the story and seem enthusiastic, then you have a good pitch! If you're looking for an unbiased opinion, try finding groups of readers and writers online and asking for their opinion on your pitch as well.

At the end of the day, figuring out how to describe your book to people can feel daunting, but the only way to get better is to practice, whether that be by writing it down or saying it out loud. I think writers naturally shy away from talking about their work, but one of the first steps of learning to market your book is being proud and confident about your story as you sell it.

BONUS TIP FROM BETHANY:

Once you have an elevator pitch, or maybe even a pretty solid idea of your blurb, it can be tough to know when to start sharing it with people. There are a few factors you could consider when trying to decide if you're ready or if you want to keep it to yourself a little bit longer...

First, ask yourself, "Is the first draft of the story finished?" and/or "Do I know exactly what's going to happen from beginning to end?" And, "If the story were to drastically change, would the pitch or blurb change as well?" If the book isn't done, or even if you're just not sure yet—and what you tell people could potentially change—you might consider holding off on sharing. Or perhaps instead of a full elevator pitch of the story, you could pitch the genre and some of your favorite elements instead. For example, before I had finished my fantasy series I might have said something like, "It's a young adult fantasy series of retellings, based on different fairy tales, with a persian culture and setting, including Jinni." This isn't revealing the actual story. So if something changes, it won't be confusing to anyone down the road, but it does allow me to still share details that might intrigue a potential reader.

On the other hand, if you do have a first draft or maybe you're even on the second, third, or fourth draft, you might have a fairly solid story and be ready to share more. At that point, the question becomes, "Is this elevator pitch and this blurb communicating my story and grabbing my reader's attention?" The only way to know that, of course, is to actually test the blurb out on others and get feedback.

You could spend a few days, a few weeks, or even a few months doing this, before you decide you're ready to share. But at some point, the question shifts from "Is the blurb ready?" to "Am I ready?" and this is when I would encourage you to set a date and be brave about sharing! You could plan to use your blurb at the same time as the cover reveal like Mandi. Or you could share as soon as you feel it's ready for the public, which is what I do. It all depends on (1) when the blurb is ready, and (2) what your strategy is for sharing. If you want to add extra excitement to the cover reveal day, the blurb could be a fantastic way to do that. Or, if you decide you want to begin building excitement as early as possible, revealing even earlier would help you do that too.

Chapter 4: Create a Publishing & Marketing Timeline

IT'S IMPOSSIBLE TO TALK about the marketing side of a book launch without also talking about the publishing side of things. When it comes to planning all your marketing leading up to release, it's imperative to also know when certain tasks on your publishing to-do list will be complete.

By far the most common question I get from authors wanting to publish is, "How long will each step in the process take?" I think everyone assumes there's a magical formula that published authors have and that we're keeping it to ourselves, refusing to share our secrets. In reality, there's no secret blueprint to publishing and marketing a book. While there's no "right way" to launch a book, we'll be using this chapter to talk about the different ways you can create a publishing and marketing timeline for yourself. We'll take the list of tasks you've come up with in chapter one and figure out how to put them on a calendar and set deadlines for yourself.

Every author's publishing and marketing timeline is different, and often that timeline changes from book to book. The process of publishing your first book will be messy. By the second book, you'll know what to expect a little more, so you'll know where to invest your time and where you shouldn't cut corners as much.

In *The Book Launch Planner*, I provide estimates for how long each step might take. For example, I estimate it might take about one month to implement edits based on feedback from beta readers. Some people may be able to get edits done faster, while other people may take three or four months to edit. And that's fine! When creating your timeline, estimate how long tasks will take based on how quickly you've worked in the past to create goals that are realistic for your book.

Discover How Long Tasks Take

To understand how long it will take you to write, edit, or do some of the bigger steps in the publishing process, it can be best to break things down, step by step. Let's say you're working with a developmental editor. Your book is 80,000 words long and you normally edit about 2,000 words a day. With that math, you'll be done editing your book in 40 days. But what if you want to finish in a month? Well now you divide 80,000 by 25 (because let's give you some days off), and you have to edit 3,200 words a day, plus you get five days off! Not too bad!

Break things down like this for every step, and always give yourself some wiggle room, in case things don't go as planned. By that, I mean days off or "buffer days." Publishing a book is a marathon, not a sprint. If you don't pace yourself, then you'll burn out before release day, which will make your book sales suffer.

Usually finalizing the book is the task that takes the most time, but some marketing tasks—like creating a book trailer or preparing for a cover reveal—can be highly time intensive as well. For large tasks like this, you'll always benefit from breaking it down into smaller chunks to see how much you need to work on that task each day to meet your deadlines.

Working Backward

If you're the type of person who loves working under pressure, you'll probably love the next suggestion, which is to work backward when creating your publishing timeline. This means that you can choose when you want your book to be published, and then create your deadlines for yourself working backward.

Say it's January and you want your book to be released in the summer. You pick July 14th as your release day. Working backward and setting deadlines for yourself, only to realize if you want your book published in July, you should already be working with a developmental editor if you want to meet your July 14th deadline. But you haven't even looked at editors yet. When that happens, it means you need to push out your release date so you have more time to meet your deadlines.

In terms of marketing, you may want to send out advanced reader copies of your book one month before release, so you need to work backward and make sure the book itself is ready to be sent to the first set of readers a month before release.

Working backward to set deadlines like this doesn't work for everyone, but may motivate you to stay on track for publishing!

The Extra Month

One of the most crushing things you can experience as an author is having to push back a release date after it has already been announced. So many things can go wrong during a book release that can force you to push back a promised release date and let readers down. For me, I had to push back the release for my second novel, *I am Mercy*, after getting line edits back from my editor. The edits were... not great. My editor added commas everywhere, but that's about it. I had to request that my editor redo the edits, which meant the release had to be pushed back.

At the time, it wasn't a huge deal. I didn't do pre-orders, so nothing happened besides me having to make some posts on social media announcing the date change. However, if you have pre-orders and have to reschedule a release, things won't go as smoothly. For example, Kindle Direct Publishing, which handles Kindle pre-orders, doesn't like when you push back release dates. You're allowed to push back your release *one time,* as long as it is *thirty* days or less, without penalty. However, if the delay is more than thirty days, you won't be allowed to do pre-orders on any other books for a full year. Later on in this book you'll understand how important pre-orders are and how not having pre-orders can mean a smaller paycheck for you.

As far as other eBook distributors, there may not always be a penalty for pushing back a release date, but no matter what, it's not something you want to do as an author because it's going to hurt your relationship with your readers. To avoid a situation like this, give yourself an extra month (or two) to get things done. This means, when you look at the publishing and marketing timeline you created for your book, you'll have an entire month before your release where your book is finished, proofread, and perfected.

Not only is this a good idea to do in case things take longer than planned, but even if things go perfectly, it means the entire month leading up to release you won't have to worry about finishing the book and can focus on promoting it! Dedicating the final month before release to marketing means you can put your best foot forward and start your book sales off with a bang!

Types of Timelines

Let's talk about my favorite part: how to organize it all! When I plan and market a book release, I have two different tools I use.

The first is *The Book Launch Planner*. I designed it with my past experiences in mind, and with the feedback from many other writers and authors. There are over fifty pages of templates and checklists in the planner that I reference to make sure I never forget anything since there are so many things to keep track of. As I publish, I'm constantly flipping through the pages to make sure I don't forget to check something off.

Now, as much as I love *The Book Launch Planner*, I also like to track everything digitally using

Google Drive. For each book I launch, I have a Google Drive folder dedicated to that book. In that folder, I have documents containing the finalized blurb, ISBNs, publishing timelines, the cover files, and anything else electronic that's related to the book. I cannot stress how important it is to have everything organized in one place. I love Google Drive because I can access it from my computer, laptop, iPad, phone, and—when I worked full time—even on my work computer (if my old boss is reading this, sorry).

I enjoy using two different timelines: a paper one (*The Book Launch Planner*) and an electronic one (Google Drive) for different reasons. I tend to lean toward the electronic one on a day-to-day basis because it's so easy to add and rearrange info, but I love *The Book Launch Planner* because the lists help me cover all the basics and make sure I'm not forgetting anything. Plus goals and deadlines feel more concrete when they're written on paper.

For the sake of giving you a better understanding of the many types of timelines you can create for yourself, let's break them all down. Once you see some of the timeline options you have, you may be able to pinpoint which tool you'll want to use to create your publishing and marketing timeline.

Timeline Tool #1: The Book Launch Planner

The timeline in *The Book Launch Planner* is straightforward. It's designed for those who like a little guidance and are always asking, "Am I forgetting something?" To make sure you don't forget a step, I break things down into the following sections:

- The Editing
- The Cover
- The Interior
- The Details
- The Set-Up
- Advanced Reader Copies
- The Marketing

Sample of timeline page from The Book Launch Planner

There's also a section that's blank if you want to add on any additional tasks.

Within each section, things are broken down further, with each additional task given a suggested estimate of how long each task might take, and how far before the release date it should happen. Again, these dates are just rough estimates to give you a vague idea of what to expect. There are boxes for each step, large enough to write down how long you'll be working on it, and the day you *need* to have the task finished by.

I like to use the planner to write down the exact date things are due, so when I need to reference it quickly, I can just flip to that page. My deadlines and due dates for publishing usually change as I go through the process, but the planner is the place where the most accurate deadlines are written down.

Timeline Tool #2: The Gantt Chart:

My personal favorite of all types of timelines is the Gantt chart because it is a very visual tool that allows you to show when tasks overlap and how long it will take you to complete the task.

In simple terms, it looks like a bar graph. On the x-axis are your tasks, and on the y-axis are the dates (you'll see an example below). When using an excel sheet (or a Google sheet in my case), each month gets four or five columns, one for each week in the month. This means when I'm filling in a specific task to figure out how long it will take, I color in the boxes of the week or weeks that I think I'll be working on it, and that gives me an idea of how long I will need.

For example, if editing takes me three weeks, then I will color in three boxes on the x-axis associated with editing.

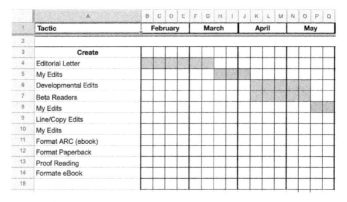

A	B	C	D	E	F	G	H	I	J	K	L	M	N	O	P	Q
1 Tactic		February				March				April				May		
2																
3 Create																
4 Editorial Letter																
5 My Edits																
6 Developmental Edits																
7 Beta Readers																
8 My Edits																
9 Line/Copy Edits																
10 My Edits																
11 Format ARC (ebook)																
12 Format Paperback																
13 Proof Reading																
14 Formate eBook																
15																

Gantt chart editing timeline sample for Meet Me at the Summit

To organize things further, I like to break my Gantt chart into three sections:

Create – This section includes all the steps that help me create the book like rewrites, specific types of edits, formatting, and cover design.

Market – This section has all the steps that have to do with marketing leading up to the release like cover reveals, advanced reader copies, street teams, and more.

Post-Release – This last section covers the marketing plans I have for after the book has been released.

A	B	C	D	E	F	G	H	I	J	K	L	M	N	O	P	Q	R	S	T	U	V	W	X	Y	Z	AA	AB	AC
Tactic		February			March			April			May			June				July			August							
Create																												
Editorial Letter																												
My Edits																												
Developmental Edits																												
Beta Readers																												
My Edits																												
Line/Copy Edits																												
My Edits																												
Format ARC (ebook)																												
Format Paperback																												
Proof Reading																												
Formate eBook																												
Market																												
Reveal Title																												
Cover Reveal Sign Up																												
Sumit book for pre-order																												
Pre-Orders - Cover, Blurb																												
Pre-Order Campaign																												
Announce Street Team																												
Start Team																												
Street Team Posts																												
Annouce ARC																												
NetGalley																			14									
NetGalley: Featured Title Spotlight																			21									
Send ARC's																												
Teaser Tuesday																												
Review Features																												
Book Trailer																												
Publication Day!																												

Sample of the "Create" and "Market" section of my Gantt chart for Meet Me at the Summit.

From there, I start filling in all my tasks by coloring in boxes of when I'd like to work on them. I also like to color code the boxes that I color in.

In the "Create" section, tasks that I need to complete are colored in purple. If it's a task *someone else* needs to do (like an editor or cover designer), then the box is blue. This way when I look at the timeline and I see the book is with my editor the entire month of January, I know I have time to work on something else.

The boxes in the marketing section get colored pink, and the release day of my book gets colored bright red. I color-code this way because I know purple tasks (creating the book) are more time consuming than pink tasks (marketing the book). The release day is red so that it sticks out and is a constant reminder of the biggest deadline I have. You can choose whatever color-coding system that works best for you, or you can choose not to use colors at all.

I usually put a specific due date that tasks are due in the last colored box, and then delete the dates after I've completed them to keep my chart cleaner and easier to read.

If you're writing a series, I would recommend duplicating the three sections once again for every book in the series. You could start a new sheet for other books, but I like to keep them all together, because the visual may help you notice possible conflicts—like if you've planned to start drafting book two while you're also supposed to be editing book one.

If you'd like to use this specific book release

Gannt chart, you can access a free download in the resources section of this book.

Timeline Tool #3: Sticky Notes:

The last timeline tool I'm going to be talking about is good, old-fashioned sticky notes! You can work with sticky notes any way you'd like, but I think the most common method is writing a task on a sticky note and moving it around on a calendar, the wall, or a large paper until it feels like all the tasks are in order. You can group your sticky notes by types of tasks, or by what month they'll be completed in. The possibilities are endless.

I find sticky notes are most useful when you're not sure where to start, so you move things around and to see how things fit. For new authors this method can be especially helpful because it's the most visual and lets you rearrange everything easier, while getting a better grasp on what tasks are ahead.

When I published my first novel, I worked only with sticky notes, but now I use both *The Book Launch Planner* and the Gantt Chart. I found working with two different types of timelines helps me remember when things are due, and also spot when there's an error in my timeline.

There are more types of publishing timelines than the ones named in this chapter. I've only mentioned the ones I use myself, but there are numerous ways to organize your publishing timeline. My best advice is to see how other authors organize themselves and try out a few different methods until you discover what works best for you. You can find authors by following them on social media, joining Facebook groups, or joining your local writing group in town. Over the years, I've learned countless things from friends that I would have never known otherwise.

BONUS TIP FROM BETHANY:

For all the planners out there, this part of planning a profitable book launch is going to be super fun! Maybe even more fun than actually putting the steps into motion. But for those of you who find this part of the process overwhelming, don't worry, you can enjoy it too!

Like Mandi said, every author works a little differently, which means there's no "right way" to plot your publishing and marketing timeline, and trying out different methods can be extremely valuable for you.

I personally have three favorites:

1. Poster board calendar
2. Google Docs calendar
3. Bullet journal

Since the first two are both calendars, I don't always use both of them, but I like to create a publishing calendar with at least one of these to get a bird's eye view of the big picture.

I started out using a poster board calendar exclusively, but these days I gravitate toward using the digital Google calendar instead. In both cases, the reason I chose these methods was for their flexibility.

The Poster Board Calendar

When I first started creating my publishing plans, I liked to create my big picture calendar on a cheap white poster board that you could buy at the dollar store. I would then use a sharpie to split it up evenly into four sections and draw out the four months leading up to my release. (Yes, you can technically buy desk calendars that already have each month neatly designed and printed, but I have never been able to find a calendar that laid out the exact four months that I needed side-by-side like this—and this is how I get my "bird's eye view" of all four months at once that I find so valuable).

Once I have the correct four months drawn out, I use the "sticky note method" that Mandi described to place different tasks on the dates where I generally think they *might* go. I'll even color-code my sticky notes too, in a similar way that Mandi color-codes her Gantt chart (planner nerds unite)!

After I start placing these sticky notes on the calendar, it helps me see where they might need to move. For example, if I find that I am needing to place five sticky notes with huge tasks all on the same date—that's a sign that I'm packing too much in and need to adjust my plan.

The Google Calendar

While I still love being able to physically plot out my release with pen and paper on the poster board, I have started to gradually move more toward using a Google Calendar. This is because the online version of the calendar offers almost the exact same benefits, but also allows me to access my publishing plan from anywhere on the go! If I think of something I want to add while doing errands, I can add it right then and there. Like the physical poster board version, a Google Calendar is very flexible. Nothing is set in stone. If you realize the dates aren't quite right and you need to move them around, it just takes one click!

The reason I personally find it valuable to start out with one of these calendar style options is because they provide a big picture view of your release and give you the ability to move tasks around. Every stage of the publishing process impacts other stages, so things will move around a LOT. But once you get everything on the calendar and your plan begins to solidify, that's when I move to my third favorite tool.

The Bullet Journal

Last, but not least, I like to take all those really big picture goals that span multiple months leading up to a release, and break them down into monthly, and then weekly, goals lists. Some people might not need this step, but for me, I find that big picture calendar a bit overwhelming for day-to-day purposes. It's sort of like an enormous to-do list shouting at me that it all needs to get done at once. Using a bullet journal to narrow down what needs to get done each month, then each week, and even each day, helps me to stay focused on just a handful of tasks instead of *all* the tasks at once. It's as simple as it sounds, and it doesn't have to be fancy. I just look at the big poster board calendar one month at a time, and make a separate to-do list for each month. Then, I narrow my focus from that month down to individual weeks, asking myself what needs to get done each week? These "weekly spreads," as they're often called in the bullet journal community, are a way to visually see all the to-do items that are happening that specific week so that you can focus on what you need to get done that week alone. Just like with the calendar, things might move around a bit. And that's okay! But I find it immensely helpful to narrow my focus from the "bird's eye" view down to the "what needs to get done today" view.

Those are my personal favorites, and I've also enjoyed the tools that Mandi listed as well! But that doesn't mean you have to use any of these. I've also heard authors enjoy other tools such as Evernote, Trello, or even something as simple as a notebook, or the notes app on your phone!

Don't be afraid to over-plan or make notes for yourself where you're unsure—it's not about making the prettiest plan but about making the most *helpful* one and keeping all of your to-do items organized and easy to access.

And as a reminder for those of you who are less comfortable with planning tools, it's not about copying someone else's method, it's about finding the right method for *you* that will keep you on track for a successful and profitable release. Some planning is necessary to make sure you don't miss deadlines or opportunities, but it doesn't have to be as detailed as ours if that's not right for you. The tools are just tools, so find the best one(s) for you, and give in to the planning frenzy!

Chapter 5: Are Pre-Orders an Effective Marketing Strategy?

TO PRE-ORDER OR not to pre-order, that is the question! Pre-orders can be a great marketing tool for authors that allow you to start making sales off your book before it is released, plus there are marketing strategies that are specific to pre-orders that we'll be talking about in this chapter. However, there may be times some authors choose not to do pre-orders. In this chapter, we'll be breaking down some of the pros and cons of having a pre-order, that way you can decide if it will be the right marketing decision for you! We'll also give some tips and tricks to increase the number of pre-orders through something called a pre-order campaign, as well as some steps to take if you decide *not* to do pre-orders.

So let's weigh out the pros and cons of pre-orders!

Pro: Get the Sale Now!

Pre-orders are a fantastic way to build excitement for your book before release day. It's also great because we know sometimes people can be very easily distracted. They may want to buy your book today, but then completely forget about it by the time release day comes around. Which is why pre-orders are an author's best friend: you can land the sale while the lead is still hot. If the ultimate goal of your book release is to sell as many copies as possible, pre-orders are a great option to start selling right away.

Con: Deadlines

To have a pre-order for your book, you need to decide on a release date for your book. This means you have to be confident in the date you select and that you'll be able to finish all your tasks in time. For myself, I like to wait until I at least get edits back from my developmental editor before I decide on a release date. Even then, I'll hold back on revealing the release date until I know for sure that my editing will be done in time. For some authors, the stress of meeting deadlines can ruin the joy in the publishing process. Like I discussed in the last chapter, you can move back the release date of your book, but it can sometimes come with consequences.

Pro: Deadlines

On the same note, some authors perform really well under deadlines. In fact, deadlines could be the only thing motivating you to keep editing your book. Without a release date, you may have no reason to finish the editing process anytime soon, so the firm deadline may be just the thing you need to stay accountable.

Con: Ranking for Lists

Perhaps the biggest and most common reason indie authors don't want to do pre-orders is to try to rank on certain bestseller lists like Amazon, USA Today, and The New York Times. To be very frank, it's incredibly hard for indie authors to make these lists. Most indie authors are successful because they make more money per book sale, whereas traditional authors make less per sale, but their sale numbers are far greater. To rank on any of these lists, you often have to sell thousands of books in one week. Some lists, like USA Today, count paperback (not eBook) pre-order sales toward release week sales number, but even then it can be very hard (though not impossible) for indie authors to hit those numbers.

How to rank on lists is very complex. Some lists count pre-orders, some don't. Some lists count eBook sales, some don't. Your first book probably won't be a bestseller. In fact, for indie authors that do hit the bestseller list, it's often because it's their tenth, twentieth, or even thirtieth book they've released.

My advice to you is not to worry about becoming a bestseller and to just do the best you can to write the book and make the money back you spent on publishing it. If you are interested in learning more about ranking on lists as an indie author, please refer to the resource section of this book. The Courtney Project, who has ranked on USA Today, can tell you more about her experience as an indie author, and how pre-orders can affect your ranking.

At the end of the day, pre-orders can often hinder your ability to rank on a best seller list, specifically the Amazon Bestseller List, because Amazon counts sales as they come in. This means for the best chance of ranking, you'll want as many sales as possible in a small period of time, like release week. Pre-orders make it harder to rank on Amazon because pre-orders often cause a slow trickle of sales building up to release day. This may not be great for making a list, but it is fantastic for making an income.

What About Amazon's Bestseller List?

Let's talk about the elephant in the room, which is ranking on Amazon. Unfortunately, the title of Amazon Bestselling Author has lost its credibility over the years. Technically speaking, an Amazon bestseller is a book that is ranking in the top 100 of *all books* on Amazon. However, Amazon isn't like USA Today or The New York Times where a specific list is published once a week. Amazon updates every hour, but even with that it can be incredibly hard to rank in the top 100 of all books on Amazon.

The title Amazon Bestseller has lost its credibility for a few reasons:

- There's no published list for top 100, only top 20.

- There's no backlog to prove it made it to the top 100.

- Amazon also has sub-categories you can rank in. It's very easy for authors to rank #1 in certain sub-categories and be considered a "bestseller," even if you only sold a small handful of books.

The categories is where things get a little fuzzy. There is an individual bestselling list for every book category on Amazon. Including some obscure categories. Not to mention, print and Kindle each have their own lists and categories. And then within each category is a new release section of the category. Meaning, you can rank #1 in new releases for Post-Apocalyptic Science Fiction on Kindle, but still be #864 in the category overall just because you happen to be the only new release in that genre for that day. You're still technically an Amazon Bestselling Author—though whether or not you're allowed to claim that title is an on-going debate. This is what I mean when I say the title has less credibility.

All this is not to say you shouldn't proudly wear the title of Amazon Bestselling Author. Heck, I love sharing the screenshot of when my books have the little orange flag under the title that says it's a bestseller in new releases, or in its category. But it's important for authors to understand how the categories work.

For some people, they only consider themselves a bestselling author on Amazon if they hit #1 in their category overall, or if they hit the top 100 for *all books* on Amazon. I think whether or not an author should use the title Amazon Bestselling Author will forever be a debate.

Going back to pre-orders, if you care about rankings, you can still rank on Amazon whether or not you decide to do a pre-order. However, you may have the best chance of ranking in your category on release day if you choose *not* to do a pre-order. Not doing a pre-order will potentially mean that you have more sales on release day than you might with a pre-order, making the odds of ranking on one of Amazon's lists higher.

One of the best parts of this Marketing for Authors series is that Bethany and I were able to experiment a lot with marketing strategies like this. One of the things we experimented with was not doing pre-orders for the first book in the series, *How Your Book Sells Itself.* We wanted to see if it would help the book rank better, and it did! We set up special newsletter email alerts for the first book in the series and it ranked #1 in its category on release day because of it. Could it have ranked #1 on release day either way? There's no way to know for sure, but it's been fun to use this marketing series as an excuse to play around with different techniques.

You may have noticed we went back to taking pre-orders again for the rest of the series because our goal shifted from ranking high to wanting to make as many sales as possible.

It's also worth mentioning, if you do pre-orders you can also rank in your category on Amazon *before* the book releases too. Sometimes if an author does a pre-order and cover reveal at the same time, that book will often rank high in its category because the cover reveal is such a high sales day.

Amazon's ranking updates every hour, so where your book sits on the ranking list is constantly changing. Whenever sales come in high amounts is when you have the best chance to rank high.

As you can see, rankings can get a little complicated when it comes to deciding to do a pre-order. For that reason, I try to deter authors away from worrying so much about ranking and focus on the other pros and cons of pre-orders when making a decision.

Next, let's talk about tips for those who want to skip pre-orders, as well as tips for those who'd like to try them.

What to Do When You Don't Want to Do a Pre-Order

Let's assume you've weighed all the pros and cons and have decided pre-orders aren't going to be the right fit for you and your book. Just because you aren't doing a pre-order doesn't mean you're going to do nothing. In place of a pre-order, you can set up a special email alert. For any instance leading up to release where you would normally promote a pre-order, instead you can promote an email alert.

Direct your excited readers to sign up for this specific email alert or your newsletter. Create a special landing page or form to fill out that will make it easy for them to sign up for this email notification. If you want to go all out, you can give incentives to sign up, like getting access to the first chapter of the book. Then, once the book releases, you email everyone to notify them and remind them that they can now purchase the book.

This email allows people not to forget about your book, while still saving all your sales for release day.

However if you choose to do a book pre-order, there are a few things I've learned as an author, that help me get through the logistical side of creating pre-orders.

Tips for eBook Pre-Orders

If you choose to do pre-orders, one of the easiest and most popular options would be to do pre-orders through Kindle Direct Publishing (KDP). KDP is my favorite print on demand distributor because they're user-friendly and have great customer service—plus they are owned by Amazon and therefore distribute to one of the biggest book retailers. In most cases, for beginner authors especially, KDP might be the only place you decide to go for pre-orders. However, if you want wide distribution for your eBook, and the ability to pre-order across all eBook platforms, you'll need to work through another distributor, such as Draft2Digital.

To start the pre-order process, you have the option to upload your files now or later. I recommend waiting to upload your eBook interior files until you have the final file. This is because I always have the fear that if I upload a draft version of the book or a "dummy file," I'll assume that it's the final version and forget to switch it out in time for release. Speaking of release, KDP requires you to upload the final version of the book 72 hours before release, so plan accordingly.

Tips for Print Book Pre-Orders

The most popular way to do pre-orders for paperback and hardcover books in the U.S. (at the time of writing this book) is through either

IngramSpark or Barnes and Noble Press—though there are other distributors that offer this as well.

I've never worked with Barnes and Noble Press for pre-orders, but I have worked with IngramSpark. I've had my paperback pre-orders go really well, and I've also had them go catastrophically wrong. When I released my children's book, copies of the book were printed and shipped months before the release date because I had done one tiny step wrong.

I'm happy to say since then, I have a better understanding of what to do to make sure a pre-order through IngramSpark goes smoothly:

1. Make sure the on-sale date of the book and the release date of the book are the same.

2. Give the book listing ten business days to appear on retailers after submitting your pre-order information and files.

3. Upload the final edition of the book to IngramSpark a minimum of ten *business* days before release.

Though Ingramspark says ten business days, I recommend that you give yourself closer to two or three weeks to be safe! If you want more details on how to do paperback pre-orders and how exactly mine have gone wrong in the past, please check out the resources section of this book.

Pre-Order Campaigns

If you decide to do pre-orders for your book, then you could benefit from doing a pre-order campaign. To put it simply, a pre-order campaign is when you give readers an incentive to buy the book. Think: bookish swag.

The idea behind a pre-order campaign is that anyone who pre-orders the book gets something exclusive for free—aka an incentive to purchase. It can be one thing, or a bunch of things. It can be something that you, the author, have to physically purchase and mail out, or it could be something electronic.

Choosing Pre-Order Campaign Incentives

You could go all out with pre-order campaigns. In fact, I saw one author give away bath bombs (that matched the book cover) to anyone who pre-ordered.

As fun as that sounds, it may not be the best financial decision. Earlier in this book, I talked about ROI (Return On Investment), and if you're giving away expensive bath bombs with every book you sell, it's very unlikely that you'll make your money back. On top of that, you also have to pay shipping to mail the bath bombs.

Please note: the bath bomb example was done by a traditionally published author, so as you can imagine their marketing budget was a little different.

Small Pre-Order Incentives

It's important to keep in mind the cost of shipping when you're mailing out pre-order campaign material. Especially if you want to open up the pre-orders internationally. I speak from experience when I say it can cost $10 or more to mail something as small as a pin internationally.

Here are some things you can mail in a regular envelope to save on shipping costs in general, and especially on international shipping:

- Bookmarks
- Signed bookplates
- Postcards

- Character art
- Thank you cards (with a personal note)
- Stickers

Free Pre-Order Incentives

My personal favorite is doing digital pre-order incentives because there is no cost to me, just time! When someone fills out the form, all they have to provide is their email and proof of purchase. Then all I have to do is email them the digital item I promised! Here are some ideas for digital pre-order incentives:

- First chapters of the book (if the book hasn't been proofread before you send it, make sure you note that so it doesn't affect reviews).
- Link to an exclusive livestream.
- Let them see character art before it's released to the public, or free downloads of printable character art.
- Share behind the scenes content (such as bonus scenes, publishing facts, the creation of things, etc).
- Share an exclusive workbook or infographic (for non-fiction books).

As long as what you're giving away is exclusive, it will give readers that much more of a reason to pre-order!

Large Pre-Order Incentives: Giveaways

Another pre-order incentive could be a giveaway, meaning anyone who pre-orders gets entered into a giveaway! This is great if you have a larger pre-order incentive you'd like to give away, but can only afford to give it to one or two people. You could still do the digital and/or small pre-order incentives mentioned earlier, but also have a "grand prize" that one or more people who pre-order can enter to win. This way everyone wins something, but only one person or a small handful of people also win the big prize(s). Big prizes can be more expensive to purchase, more expensive to ship, or both.

Here are some ideas for big prizes:

- Book themed candle.
- Book themed bath bomb.
- Book sleeve (that matches the cover of your book).
- Notebook with your book's cover.

- Signed edition of the book.
- A box set of previous books you've published.
- A bundle of books from other authors in the same genre as you who you'd like to support
- iPad, Nook, or Kindle Reader.
- Amazon Gift Card (or Gift Card to another retailer).

As long as it's exciting and something that can't be easily bought, it gives people reason to want to enter the giveaway and encourages more pre-orders.

Collecting Pre-Order Information

I wish I could say Amazon tracks everything for us and sends us the emails of everyone who pre-orders, but they don't. If you want to give out incentives for pre-orders, you have to track it yourself.

I've found the easiest thing to do is to create a Google Form that readers fill out, where they include their name and email and/or mailing address. The most important part of the form is that you need some way to prove they bought your book. Google Forms allow people to attach images. So whenever I do a pre-order campaign, I request that the person filling out the form attaches a screenshot of their receipt. This allows me to see that they bought the book, but readers can still crop the image enough to block out any sensitive information.

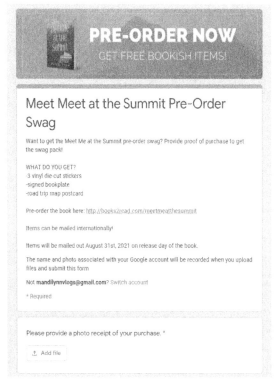

Sample of pre-order campaign form for Meet Me at the Summit

When you promote your pre-order campaign

online, make sure to always share the link to the form they need to fill out to also get whatever pre-order incentives you're giving out. In the form, I also like to paste a link to purchase the book to make it easy to buy, then click back to the form to provide proof of purchase.

When Should You Start Taking Pre-Orders?

Print on demand companies let you take pre-orders anywhere from a few days, weeks, months, or sometimes even years before the book is released. Personally, I like to wait until the three-month range to start taking pre-orders for a few reasons.

1. **Burnout** – When I market for a release, I go hard. I'd much rather have a strong three months of marketing rather than a year's worth of marketing where I get burnt out before release day.

2. **Timeline** – I like to plan as much as I can, but my timeline might take longer than I think. Three months before release I usually have a pretty good idea of whether or not I'll be able to release a book on time.

Three months before release is also when I reveal the cover of my book, which is a great way to build excitement and begin pre-orders. One thing I see a lot of authors do, is that they reveal their book cover before the pre-order is available. If you choose to do pre-orders, then I highly suggest that you wait to reveal your cover until you have your pre-order set up as well. So many authors get so excited to have their cover, that they reveal it right away. But revealing your cover is the perfect time to start getting your first sales! Take full advantage of the excitement of the cover reveal. We'll go into more detail on how to make the most of your cover reveal in the next chapter.

How to Utilize Incentives Even if You Don't Do Pre-Orders

Like I mentioned earlier, the pre-order for my children's book, *Mr. Moon's Big Move*, had a few kinks in the plan. This meant I had to cancel the pre-order campaign I had planned. What I did instead was use all of those incentives for the week of release. Anyone who ordered the book within the first week of release could fill out the form and get the cute Moon-themed stickers mailed to them! The best part of self-publishing is that there aren't rules to what you can and cannot do, so experiment with things! Feel free to do a pre-order incentive *and* a purchase incentive the first week of release. Or do neither. It's up to you!

BONUS TIP FROM BETHANY:

I've tried almost every possible version of pre-orders—or skipping pre-orders—that exists. With my debut novel, I didn't even know pre-orders were an option, so I set up a kickstarter page as a way to get early orders of my books instead. With later releases, I tried pre-orders as short as one week and as long as nine months, with other time frames in-between such as three months and six months. Like Mandi mentioned, when we began this non-fiction series, we also tried skipping pre-orders altogether and utilizing an email alert instead.

I have a lot of experience through trial and error, and I can confidently say that my favorite method as an indie author is to always set up a pre-order.

The length of time still varies for me, depending on my needs and plans for each specific book. But the reason I'm a huge advocate of pre-orders is really built into what Mandi has described in this chapter already. Pre-orders might make it harder to make it onto a bestsellers list (because those lists typically require thousands of sales within a short time frame), but pre-orders also tend to help an indie author make more money in the long run. For me, if it's a choice between an outward ranking or actual income, I would definitely prefer income (and knowing that more readers are finding my books as well). This is often referred to as "bank over rank."

Even if ranking on a list never came into play, I'd still be an advocate of pre-orders. Why? Because they train the online algorithms how to better sell your book! This is especially proven when it comes to Amazon, which has one of the most high tech AI's in existence. With each new purchase, the AI gets a better understanding of who your target reader is, and then they will show your book to other, similar readers. This type of exposure is incredibly valuable.

This is why, even though I've tested out skipping pre-orders, I will always utilize pre-orders in the future whenever possible.

Again, pre-orders give you a chance to make more sales. As an indie author, many of us are trying to build a successful career out of writing and publishing, and a huge part of that requires a solid, consistent income. The longer a pre-order lasts, the more chances you have to talk about the book and make early sales, so it stands to reason that longer pre-orders equal more income. If you had to choose between a very tiny chance at making a bestsellers list or the opportunity to make more money, for most indie authors, that decision seems pretty easy!

Chapter 6: Make the Most of Your Cover Reveal

WELCOME TO THE second most exciting day in the book launch process: cover reveal day! (The most exciting day being release day.) Cover reveals are my favorite part of the publishing process, though as a cover designer myself, I'm partial. Covers are a way of bringing your book to life, and it usually isn't until you have your cover that the reality of your book being published starts to come to fruition.

In this chapter, we're going to be covering a few

different things, like when to reveal the cover, tying it in with pre-orders, and how to get people to help share the cover (and pre-order) on social media.

Besides release day, the day you reveal your cover is the best marketing day for your book and your best chance to make sales. Cover reveal day is the day you need to promote the heck out of your book. If you plan well, you can have an entire team of people sharing your book cover and promoting the book's pre-order.

Your Cover Reveal Team

Cover reveals can be huge and exciting, or they can be just one simple post you make on social media. You get to decide how big you want it to be, but assuming your goal is to sell as many books as possible, let's assume we're going big and you want to create a team of people to help with the reveal. To form a cover reveal team, recruit as many people as possible. Post on social media that you're looking for people to help reveal the cover of your book, and to sign up all they need to do is fill out a form.

I like to use Google forms because it's free and simple to set up. When you create your form, all you need ask for is their email address. It's that simple. You can collect other information as well, like social media links and so on, but when it comes to revealing your cover, you don't need to be picky. When I do cover reveals, anyone can take part. You just need an email to send them the cover and reveal information.

On your form, also make sure you tell them what day the cover is being revealed so they can plan accordingly. Let them know when you'll be emailing them the cover and if you plan on providing them graphics.

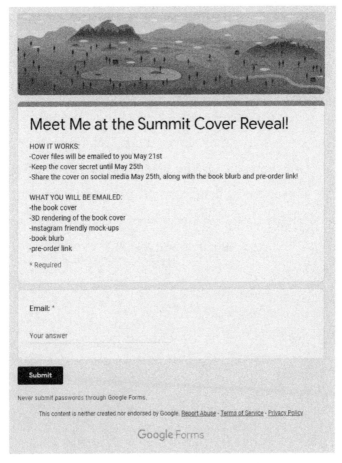

Cover reveal form I used for Meet Me at the Summit.

Post about your cover reveal everywhere and give yourself a few weeks to form a team. In the meantime, to encourage people to sign up, I like to create a teaser graphic where only a portion of the cover is revealed, giving just enough of a glimpse that people want to see the cover even more. You can create graphics like this using a website called BookBrush.

Teaser graphic for Meet Me at the Summit

How to Get People to Sign Up

People always ask me, "How do I get people to sign up when I don't have a large social media platform?" First and foremost, it's not the size of your social media following that matters, but how engaged they are. Second, as long as you have engaged followers, they'll sign up. People sign up to do cover reveals for three reasons:

- They want to support the author.
- It's easy to post the cover on social media.
- They want to see the cover!

The biggest perk of signing up for a cover reveal is that you get to see the cover before anyone else. Promote the heck out of this fact that if you sign up for the cover reveal team, you get to see the cover *early*! Seeing the cover early is key to getting people to sign up.

Giving Them Graphics to Share

A fool-proof way of making sure that as many people share the cover as possible is by giving them multiple graphics to choose from and share. Now, I'll be honest with you, just because someone signs up for a cover reveal doesn't mean they're guaranteed to share your cover online. Sometimes people sign up just to see the cover early. Annoying, yes, but inevitable. The best way to get as many shares as possible is to make sharing the cover super easy by creating a folder of graphics with the cover.

Creating Shareable Graphics

When you're prepping for your cover reveal, you're going to want to create multiple graphics that are easy to share across social media. Make graphics in different sizes, such as for Instagram, Twitter, Facebook, or whatever platform is most prominent to you. Because my main social media platform is Instagram, I make mostly square graphics, as well as some that are sized for Instagram stories.

Now, what do these graphics look like? Most of them look like they're made for Bookstagram, meaning the photos are very aesthetically pleasing and have my book placed into the shot. You can take photos yourself using a proof copy of your book to photograph, or you can create a book mock-up using tools like Canva, Photoshop, BookBrush, etc.

Here's a list of the types of graphics you might want to provide to your cover reveal team:

- Just the cover, in case someone wants to create their own graphic.
- A 3D rendering of the book with a

transparent background.

- The cover of the book with pretty backgrounds that match the cover.
- A digital rendering of the book on a Kindle, Nook, or phone.
- The cover and a background with text such as "pre-order now," or the release date, or other useful info.
- A picture of someone reading the book.
- Other Bookstagram worthy photos, such as book flatlay photos, the book on a shelf, with a cup of coffee, sitting on a desk, etc.

You get the idea. Below are some examples of graphics that I've created:

3D rendering with transparent background

Cover with a background and important text

Book flatlay

Someone reading the book

Book sitting on a table

How to Send Graphics to Your Cover Reveal Team

Once you have all the graphics, you can compile them all into a Google Drive folder (or a similar platform), and share the link to the folder with everyone who signed up! It's best to give the files to everyone a handful of days ahead of time so they can prepare, but not too early that they forget when the actual cover reveal date is. I like to think one or two days ahead of time is a good range.

When you email everyone who signed up, don't forget to include the following information in the email:

- A link to the file with all the graphics.
- The pre-order link.
- The description of the book (both a long description and short description, if you have them).
- The release date.
- And above all, a reminder *not* to share until the specified date and time!

Cover Reveal Tour

For your cover reveal, you can keep it simple or choose to go all out with a cover reveal tour. This could mean hiring people to help out or putting together a tour on your own.

One of the most popular options as of publishing this book is to run an Instagram tour, meaning that for a set amount of time (usually a week or so), a different Bookstagram account will feature your book each day to promote the cover and pre-order. Where your cover reveal tour happens can vary. In the past, virtual cover reveal tours often took place on blogs, as well as on Facebook. No matter the platform, the process for a cover reveal tour is usually the same.

For Instagram, there are companies you can hire to arrange the tour for you. They usually have a long list of Bookstagrammers at their disposal, and most of those Bookstagrammers have large followings. While I love this option, it can often be expensive. There are cheaper companies you can work with, but cheap usually means the Bookstagrammers sharing your book will have smaller followings. For a list of popular tour companies, there will be a blog post by Day Leitao in the resources section of this book.

There are two big pros to hiring a company for an Instagram tour, the first being the exposure. You can get your book in front of people who would have otherwise never heard of your book, and hopefully get a few sales.

The second pro is that you will get a lot of amazing photos out of the process. Each Bookstagram account will create an aesthetically pleasing photo featuring your book that you can re-share to your account.

The first con is that it is practically impossible to measure the return on investment. You could get 100 pre-orders, but who can say whether or not they came from the Instagram tour? You can see how many people liked or commented on the photos, but that doesn't mean the sales came from that post.

The second con is the fact that most large Instagram tour companies don't want to work with indie authors. Most tour companies and the Bookstagrammers that work with the tour companies do well because the books they feature are traditionally published. This is usually because tour companies don't want to vet indie authors to decide if the book is good enough to be featured.

The third con is that usually you will be required to mail copies of the book to the Bookstagrammers. Most Bookstagrammers know how to digitally add the book into their photos using Photoshop or another tool like BookBrush, but some will still prefer to have the physical book to take photos and read. The cost of buying and shipping books to multiple people is something that adds up very quickly.

Deciding to work with a tour company is a personal decision, but know if you do, you have to go in with the possibility of it costing you more than what it makes you.

Remember that you could also find and contact reviewers yourself and plan a tour on your own! This means you would have to reach out to book reviewers yourself to see if they're willing to feature your book. Arranging a tour yourself is a budget-friendly option, but keep in mind that you're in charge of making sure everyone features the book on a different date, which makes for a lot of back and forth.

Working with a tour company means you'll usually have access to reviewers with larger audiences, while setting up a tour on your own will more often mean working with smaller accounts or accounts of a similar size to your own.

What you do for your cover reveal is entirely up to you! The planning of it can be a little stressful, making sure you've checked off all your to-do's before the cover goes live, but I promise you, this is one of the most fun steps in the publishing process, because for an entire day all everyone can talk about is how much they love your cover and that they can't wait to read the book!

BONUS TIP FROM BETHANY:

Like everything else in this book, you've probably noticed that there are a about a million options when it comes to cover reveals. You can reveal little pieces at a time, such as an elevator pitch, the blurb, the release date, a sneak peek of a piece of the cover, a goodreads page, and then finally the cover (and hopefully pre-order link!). Or you could go all in, in a big flash, and reveal everything in one exciting day!

There's no "right" way, so some things to consider are: (1) advice from other authors with experience, and (2) what would be the best fit for you personally.

If the idea of trying to juggle all the reveals and share everything at once sounds stressful to you, then take it slow and just share one thing at a time! No one is rushing you. But if the idea of stretching everything out and holding onto secrets for *so* long sounds awful, and you'd rather spill all the exciting news as soon as possible, go for it!

When it comes to bringing other people onto your cover reveal team, I have two thoughts: (1) Yes, it will make it more stressful, without a doubt. Possibly more expensive as well, if you choose to hire help, such as a graphic artist for the images, or a tour team. But (2) it will extend your reach so much further than you could ever reach on your own! Instead of shouting from your own singular rooftop, you could get dozens of other excited readers to also shout from their own rooftops—just imagine how much further the news of your book could travel!

It doesn't have to be all or nothing, though. Maybe you decide to skip the cover reveal team and just send the cover reveal information and graphics to your newsletter on release day. You could invite them to share without the pressure of forming a specific team prior to the big day—I've done this and had great success! Many readers will see the building excitement or want to support you, and they'll decide to join in, even without a prior commitment.

Or maybe you decide to hire out, but you don't want to overspend your marketing budget, so you go with a smaller (but still reputable!) company with a smaller reach—that's still going to be more reach than you would have had on your own!

I've worked with a company that created an Instagram tour for me for a fee multiple times, and I've also created my own similar tour for free (spending time instead of money) multiple times as well. I can say from experience that whatever you choose to do, if you involve more people, it will help the news of your cover reveal and upcoming release spread further than you ever could on your own.

But don't put too much pressure on yourself to do this "perfectly." A cover reveal in many ways is just one grand experiment to see how your book will do. It is not the "be all, end all", but rather, the first of many marketing adventures! So invest the time and energy that you can into making it your personal best, and then continue on to the next steps, because your release promotion is far from over!

Chapter 7: Form a Street Team

WHEN YOU'RE AN indie author, one thing you want most of all is help promoting your book, and that's exactly what a street team is for. Your street team's job, first and foremost, is to promote your book. Street team is a marketing term for a group of people who "hit the streets" to market something. In the book world, it means they're readers talking to other readers. They're already inside the community of people you want to market to, and they help you on a voluntary basis. You can give them tasks, bounce ideas off of them, and have people to talk to on a more personal level about your book during the publishing process.

A street team is not required during the publishing process. In fact, I've only used a street team once before to publish a book, but it's a valuable tool that can be used. A lot can go into the decision of whether or not you want to have a street team during the book release. The biggest factor is how much time you're willing to invest in your team. As we work through this chapter, you'll notice a lot goes into a street team, so take that into account when deciding if this is a good marketing tactic for you.

What to Call Your Street Team

I've come across a handful of people who don't like the term street team, probably because it sounds too corporate, but it's not so much the name that matters, as what you do with your team. I personally still like to use the term street team because it's widely understood what it means. But you can call your team anything. In fact, I think it's even more fun if you can give your street team a unique name that fits your brand or the theme of your book.

Creating Your Street Team

Creating your street team starts the same way it will for any group you want to create: post about it on social media and/or your newsletter. Give yourself a few weeks to post about it, and even educate your audience on what a street team is. Just because someone doesn't know the term, doesn't mean they wouldn't make a good member. Post about the benefits of a street team and your plan to create a small community of people to promote the book.

Google Forms, or a similar platform, can be used to collect responses from people interested in joining your street team. In the form, you'll want people to fill out information about themselves so you can get a good idea of who could be a good fit. Here are examples of things you can ask for in the form:

- Name.
- Email.
- Have they read your past books? If so, did they like them?
- What genres do they usually read in?
- What genres do they dislike?
- Links to their social media platforms and websites.

The goal of these types of questions is to see if they'd like your book. If their least favorite genre is horror and your book has horror elements, you probably won't want them on your team. You also want to ask for their social media account because at the end of the day, this is all about marketing your book. You can only have so many people on your street team. If you're trying to choose between two people who both seem like a good fit, you're going to want to choose the person with the higher follower and engagement rate. Notice I also said engagement rate. Number of followers doesn't mean as much as it used to. If your choice for the final person on your street team is between two people who have a similar number of followers, then choose the person whose posts get more comments and likes. Big follower numbers are great, but they mean nothing if their posts don't get engagement from their community.

How Many People Should be on Your Team?

Street teams are hard to form, so sometimes you

end up accepting everyone who applies, which isn't a bad thing! But there may be other times where you feel like too many people applied, and that there's no way you can have every single person on your street team. So how many people should you choose?

This is a hard question to answer because it comes down to personal preference and what you want your team to be like. You may think the bigger the better, but sometimes a smaller team is better. Here are some pros and cons to each:

Large street teams:

- Pro: There's power in numbers. The more team members, the larger reach you have.

- Pro: If you aren't able to constantly interact with the team, they can interact with each other and form a community.

- Con: The larger the team, the less one-on-one time you have with everyone. Sometimes the more one-on-one attention you give to your street team, the more engaged they will be, and the better results you'll get.

Small street teams:

- Pro: You get to form a better relationship with your team, and as a result, the team tends to put more effort into tasks because they are more engaged

- Pro: Sometimes the small groups allow you to get to know people better and potentially meet new friends or even potential beta readers or critique partners.

- Con: There are less people promoting your book.

What makes a street team work is not the numbers, but the community that is formed. Your street team will put more time and passion into marketing your book if you work closely with them, and you can't do that if you have a huge street team. Yet on a same note, a team of five people won't be nearly as effective as a team of ten people. It's usually best if you can find a sweet spot in the middle: a team that's not too small, but not so large that members get lost in a sea of people either. Engage with your team and give them a reason to market the book.

I've found my magic number for street team members is fifteen because I feel like it's small enough that I can manage everyone, but still large enough that if some people don't interact, it's not the end of the world. Just like a cover reveal, some people will sign up intending to interact in the street team, but things come up. Odds are, there will be a small handful of people in your street team that don't engage with the group, and that's fine.

At the end of the day, you have to decide for yourself how big you want your street team to be, and a lot of it depends on how much time you want to invest into it. If you feel like you won't have a lot of time, you might be better off having a larger team, so that way at least the team members can interact with each other when you aren't there.

Where to Host Your Team

Once you have your team picked out, you have to notify everyone about whether or not they've been picked! I usually do this by email, reaching out to everyone one by one. I like to host my street teams over Facebook groups, but you can host on any group platform you'd like as long as it allows the entire group to interact with each other and share content like photos. Other options include Discord, WhatsApp, and so on. Whatever platform you choose, it's a good idea to mention it when people sign up, so members aren't blind-sided if, for example, they realize they have to make a Discord account and they have no clue how to use Discord.

You can also host your street team through emails, but it's not as personal because the other street team members never get to meet each other, and they're only ever talking to you.

Schedule Posts for Your Team

I'm notoriously bad at keeping up with my street team. In the middle of book launches there's so much going on that I often get too caught up in everything else to connect with my team. The main reason I like Facebook is because I can schedule out my posts. I can dedicate an entire day to pre-scheduling everything, and then just make notes to myself to check in throughout the week and interact with everyone. Sometimes the best way to keep your street team motivated to market your book is by interacting with them.

When I have a street team, I have weekly tasks. These tasks aren't meant to be homework, but a way for me to constantly engage with my team. Some of the tasks are to help market the book, while other tasks are fun ways for my team to interact with each other in the group. Below are examples of tasks I give to my street team to either market my book, and also to myself to engage with my team so they continue to interact in the group.

Tasks for Street Team Members to Help Market Your Book

- Read the Advanced Reader Copy.
- Review the book on Goodreads.
- Post the review on your blog or social media platform of choice.
- Share your favorite quote from the book on social media.
- Brainstorm ideas for fun things to do on the book's release day.
- Cosplay a character.
- Create fan art.
- Post about the book on release day.
- Write a review on Amazon.

Please note: when you give your street team tasks, it's beneficial to give due dates. This lets your team know when you'd prefer a task to be finished by. There's no repercussions if they don't finish on time, or if they aren't able to do the task at all, but due dates help keep people accountable, so they don't fall behind.

Tasks for You to Engage with Your Street Team

- Play two truths and a lie, or other ice-breaker games.
- Ask your team questions that have to do with the book, such as:
  - If you were [character's name] what would you have done in [scene]?
  - What's your favorite location in the book?
  - Which character do you relate to most?
  - Was there a plot twist you never saw coming?
- Host a private livestream and answer questions about the book.

- Share behind the scenes content of the publishing process.

Plan Posts Ahead of Time

Ideally you want to have a post planned for your street team once or twice a week. I like to rotate my posts between marketing posts and engagement posts. That way I feel like I'm not being too task-oriented while still keeping everyone interested in the group and having fun!

In *The Book Launch Planner*, there are pages dedicated to coming up with task ideas for your team and creating a schedule for the tasks/posts you're going to make. I find planning ahead is the best way to keep yourself and your team on track!

Example of one of the street team pages in The Book Launch Planner

I like to write down ideas for all my posts, as well as graphics to share with each post, because my team will be more likely to see it and engage with the post if there are visuals. Sometimes the graphic I use is a graphic that they can screenshot and reshare on social media, so it's a win-win!

Creating graphics for your street team is huge! While your street team will sometimes make their own photos and graphics to promote the book, if you create graphics that are easy to share, they are more likely to use them, resulting in more book sales!

Street Team Giveaways

Sometimes you can help motivate your team to market your book by hosting giveaways. For every task you have, you can have a mini-giveaway. For example, if a task is to make character art, every street team member that creates character art would be entered into a giveaway and one random winner would be chosen. This is a great way to motivate your team to finish tasks on time. However, doing giveaways isn't always cost effective, so you have to make that decision yourself.

The only time you *can't* do a giveaway is when you're asking people to review your book. Not only does hosting a giveaway go against Amazon's review terms of service, but it takes away the whole point of writing an honest and unbiased review.

If you decide to do a giveaway for other tasks, you can use the same types of giveaway ideas we talked about for pre-orders, such as:

Small items:

- Bookmarks
- Signed bookplates
- Postcards
- Character art
- Thank you cards (with a personal note)
- Stickers

Large items:

- Book-themed candle.
- Book-themed bath bomb.
- Book sleeve (that matches the cover of your book).
- Notebook with your book's cover.
- Signed edition of the book .

- Previous book(s) you've published.
- A bundle of books from other authors in the same genre as you who you'd like to support.

Free Items:
- Bonus chapters.
- Other downloadables.

When to Form Your Street Team

You don't want to start your street team too early before release because you might run out of content and the team could fizzle out before the book release.

I like to form my street team two or three months before release. This allows the team to read the book, have fun promoting it, and see some behind the scenes of the publishing process.

Your street team usually ends the week the book is released. You'll want to visit your street team on release day, reminding them to review the book on Amazon. After that, the street team's tasks are usually done. Some authors keep their street teams after release, especially if the team worked well together and there's another book coming out in the series. Either way, after release make sure to thank everyone for all their hard work!

BONUS TIP FROM BETHANY:

If street teams sound super overwhelming to you, then I have good news—you don't have to set up a street team to be successful. I have never actually done a street team myself! There were times I considered it and one instance where I was about to work with a team, but in the end, I never have.

Does that mean that I market my books all by myself and don't get help from anyone? Absolutely not! In many ways, I have treated my newsletter subscribers as a sort of "mini-street team" and received similar help from them in promoting my books.

Obviously, I don't approach this quite the same way, since I would never want to assume that every single person on my newsletter is an advocate for my book, the way you could assume someone on a street team would be, who signed up specifically for that purpose. So I would not usually give my newsletter any direct "challenges" or push them to do anything they didn't want to do. I do however give them early access to the cover and ask for their help sharing—

that sounds like a street team activity, right? I also share extra graphics like Mandi described and encourage them to post about the book if they'd like. As a release gets closer, I like to include some chapter sneak peeks in my newsletter, plus other fun facts about the book like quotes or early reviews, and of course the links to Goodreads and all vendors where the book is for sale. Each time I do this, I encourage them to share their excitement about the book too.

Your newsletter is not going to be a set group of people that you can count on, the way you would your street team, but you would be surprised how many of your readers will be more than happy to support you! And the flexibility of utilizing your newsletter subscribers (and followers on social media in general as well) is that while they might not participate in every big announcement or post, there are usually enough excited people to generate a similar amount of buzz for your books.

Again, I would not treat your newsletter or social media following with the same intensity as an official street team, but if you're not feeling ready to build an official group or you don't have the time to invest in that right now, just know that you can still encourage your current supporters to hype your book by being excited about it yourself and sharing similar content/graphics with your newsletter (and even the public sometimes) as you would with your street team!

Chapter 8: Send Advance Reader Copies

AN ARC, ALSO known as an Advanced Reader Copy, is a version of the book you send out to reviewers to start building buzz for the book before it is released. This is how books are able to get review quotes for promotional purposes long before the book comes out. It's also a great way to start building up reviews on Goodreads before release day. Word of mouth is a huge marketing tool and readers love seeing what other readers have to say about a book before they buy, which is why collecting reviews is so important.

ARCs are copies of the book you give out for free in exchange for an honest review. An ARC is sometimes an uncorrected proof copy, meaning it hasn't been proofread yet. If it's not a corrected copy, you need to make that clear when you are giving out Advanced Reader Copies. With that said, if you are able to use a final corrected edition of your book for ARCs, that would be better.

ARCs are technically allowed to have typos, but depending on the amount of typos, it can affect the reader's ability to enjoy the story, and therefore the review of the book. Unfortunately, I speak from experience. For my newest novel, *Meet Me at the Summit*, I had the opportunity to have my book featured on NetGalley (a platform traditional publishers use to distribute ARCs) for a week, but it had to be before I had my final round of proofreading. Since this was my only option to be featured, I took it, assuming the copy edits I had done were enough.

It was after reviews started coming in and my proofreader started going through my book, that I realized a lot of things had been missed in the copy edits. The result was review after review on

NetGalley stating that the book had typos and other errors that were in need of fixing, even though nearly all these reviewers enjoyed the story itself.

The good news is that I had the ability to contact everyone, apologize for the typos, and provide them with the final edition of the book. But that situation is not one you want to be in as an author, so take the time to make your ARC as clean as possible. Get at least one round of proofreading in before sending out ARCs, and if possible, send out final editions of the book to be as professional as possible.

For most indie authors, you will send ARCs in eBook form. Yes, you could mail printed copies of your Advanced Reader Copies, but it's not cost effective. To break it down, printing just 10 books can cost you $40 or more, depending on the book's size. To ship it in the United States is usually somewhere around $4 each, but if you need to ship internationally it could be anywhere from $15-$60. Paperback ARCs are almost never worth it in my opinion. Sometimes book bloggers will require physical copies of the book to be featured on their blog or social media. In cases like this, you have to weigh out the pros and cons, and decide if the price of printing and shipping the book will be worth the feature online.

We'll be talking about how to send out ARCs and who to send them to shortly, but let's talk about how to create your ARC next, whether it be an eBook or paperback.

How to Create an eBook ARC

Now, of course, before you can send any ARCs you have to have your eBook files ready to go! You could technically email reviewers a Microsoft Word document or PDF. This makes it easy for your book to be pirated, so I like to sway authors away from that option.

Like always, there are many different ways to create your eBook files. Here are a few options:

1. Format the eBook in Microsoft Word and convert using Calibre.
2. Format the eBook in Microsoft Word and convert using Draft2Digital.
3. Format the eBook in InDesign and convert using Calibre (InDesign only gives you an ePub file, not MOBI).

As you can see, there's conversion involved in

every option. Personally, my favorite option—unless your book has a lot of photos or sub-headers (like this book)—is to do option two.

For option one and two, you're formatting your eBook first in Microsoft Word. Make it obvious where your chapter headers are by making the fonts big and bold. From there you can upload the Word document to Calibre or Draft2Digital and it will convert it into an eBook.

Calibre (which is a free software) is a little tricky because besides uploading the book, it doesn't really do anything else. While you can see where you went wrong, you can't correct it within the software itself. Instead, you have to correct the Word document, and then upload it again to see if you fixed it.

Draft2Digital is a little easier because they let you tweak some things, and also add front and back matter to your eBook, directly on the website. Draft2Digital also has a few decorative options for your eBook, which is always a win!

I have a few tutorials on YouTube (and so does Bethany) on how to format eBooks, so you can find the link to those in the resource section of this book.

For the third option, you have to have access to Adobe InDesign, which is a professional graphic design software used for books, flyers, newspapers, eBooks and so on. This is the software I use when I format books for my clients and it's a dream to work with, but only if you know how to use it! However, InDesign only lets you export as ePub, meaning if you also want to send ARCs to a Kindle email, you will need your book as a MOBI file as well. This is why I use Calibre to easily convert the ePub file to a MOBI file.

How to Create a Paperback ARC

In most cases your ARC will be an eBook, but if you want to send paperback ARCs there are some things you need to know. Kindle Direct Publishing is my favorite print on demand company, but it definitely has its downsides, one of which being that when you print copies of the book before release day, they put a big "NOT FOR RESALE" graphic across the cover. This is fine for personal needs, such as when you're proofreading the book, but if you want to give out paperback ARCs this is an issue because it won't look good for photos, and it can appear unprofessional.

To get paperback ARCs that look like the final copy, you can print your book through another print on demand company, such as IngramSpark or Barnes and Noble Press. To differentiate between the published version and the ARC version, I also like to put a sticker on the book to mark it as an ARC—not only for readers to be aware, but also so I don't get it mixed up with the final copies. The sticker acts in the same way as KDP's "NOT FOR RESALE" stamp across the front, but it covers less of the cover and it looks more professional. Again, I recommend that you avoid sending ARCs that haven't been proofread, but if you choose to go this route, a sticker on the cover serves as a reminder that this book is not the final edition, and that it's possible it has typos.

She's Not Here *with an "Uncorrected Proof" sticker to mark it as an ARC.*

Distributing Your ARCs

There are many ways you can distribute your eBook ARCs, and they vary depending on how much time you want to dedicate into it and how much money you're willing to spend. Here are some examples:

- **Ask your followers on social media/your newsletter** - Create some kind of form (like a Google Form) where people can sign up and you choose who gets an ARC and who doesn't. Send the eBook to everyone manually one-by-one.

- **Reach out to bloggers/influencers** - Contact people who review books regularly and have a social media presence, and ask if they'd be willing to read and review your book. Before you contact them, make sure the books they currently read are similar to yours, to make sure they're a good fit. For those that agree to read, manually send the book to everyone one-by-one.

- **PR Company Tour**- Similar to the Instagram Tour companies we talked about in chapter six, you can also hire a tour company that has access to bloggers/reviewers to read and review your book. In this case, you don't have to do any of the contacting to ask if they want to review, but it's usually your job to make sure that the bloggers/reviewers have a copy of your book, whether that be digital or physical.

- **NetGalley** - Netgalley is a website that publishers use to send out advanced copies. As an author or publisher, you have to pay to have your book listed on this website, but it's a great way to appear more professional and access a whole new set of readers. Readers can download the book directly through the website, and NetGalley also reminds readers to review on release day. Over the years, NetGalley has added more reasonably priced options for indie authors where you can pay by the month, when previously you could only pay for a six-month listing. Along with having your book listed on the website, you can also pay to have your book featured on the website.

- **StoryOrigin** – StoryOrigin is a website similar to NetGalley that handles the distribution of the ARC eBooks for you, but it's designed with indie authors in mind. There's both a free and a paid plan, but most authors can get by with the free option. The downside to StoryOrigin is that you have to promote your book yourself by sharing the link so people can apply for the ARC. You don't have to manually email the eBook to everyone, but unlike NetGalley, there isn't a backlog of readers looking for the next book to discover either. Another issue I've come across with StoryOrigin is that you don't have direct access to your reviewers. If half your ARC readers don't write a review, you can't email them unless they posted their review to StoryOrigin, which can make following up impossible.

How to Send eBook ARCs

There are other ways to send eBook ARCs, but I'm going to break down my three favorite options in more detail:

1. Manually through Kindle.
2. Automatically through StoryOrigin.
3. And automatically through NetGalley.

Sending ARCs Manually Through Kindle

1. Ask for the reviewer's Kindle email address associated with their account. If you set up a Google form for ARCs, this is a good question to include in your form.

2. Ask the reviewer to add your personal email (not your Kindle email, but the email you'll use to

send the file) to their safe senders list. To learn how to add an email as a safe sender, a link with instructions will be in the resources section of this book.

3. Attach your eBook's MOBI files to an email. Delete all content within the body of the email, as well as the subject line, and then send the email to the reviewer's Kindle address.

As long as your email was added as a safe sender, the eBook will load into their Kindle device! While I love this option, there are obviously a lot of steps. Now imagine trying to do this ten times with ten different people. It can get a bit tedious. However, if you plan on sending it to only a few people here and there, this is a quick, easy option.

Sending ARCs Automatically Through StoryOrigin

StoryOrigin is a fantastic tool and it has so many options for authors, but one of my favorite options is the Advanced Reader Copy process. Readers can apply through a form, and then you pick and choose who gets ARCs. As you approve readers, they are automatically notified, and StoryOrigin allows them to choose which format they want to read their eBook in, which means they aren't limited to just Kindle.

How to Create ARC Copies in StoryOrigin

1. After you create a StoryOrigin account, go to the "Review Copies" tab and select "Create a Review Copy."

2. Fill out all the information and upload a sample of your book. I like to upload the first three chapters, or whatever I feel will leave the reader wanting more. Readers can read the sample files to decide if the book is a good fit for them. There is also a spot to upload the full manuscript of your book, but the full manuscript is only sent to readers that you accept. The eBook file types required for upload include MOBI, ePub, and PDF (PDF is optional).

3. You will be given a link to share that allows readers to apply to read the ARC.

4. As people apply, you can look through applications to see where readers are willing to review (Amazon, Goodreads, their blog, and so

on). They can also let you know if they read the book sample and provide links to their website and social media. Once you hit accept, the reader will be emailed a link to download the full book.

5. On release day, log into StoryOrigin and go back to the "Review Copies" tab. Under the title of your book you will see an option to "Mark Published." Select that button and anyone you accepted as an ARC reader will be emailed a reminder to review the book on Amazon.

Readers also have the option to upload their reviews to StoryOrigin to show you where they've left their reviews. When you select "View accepted applicants" you can see these stats, as well as who hasn't reviewed, when they were reminded to review, and so on! You can find a full tutorial on this process by visiting the resources section of this book.

This option is usually a favorite for indie authors because it's free, automated, and relatively easy to set up. The downside is that readers also have to have a StoryOrigin account to apply, so that may deter readers. And like I mentioned earlier, you only get direct access to reader's emails If they post a review of the book to StoryOrigin. So if they forget to write a review for the book, there's no way to follow up and remind them.

The Pros and Cons of NetGalley

As I write this, I'm still learning about the pros and cons of having my book listed on NetGalley. I hesitate to write about the experience in this book at all because it's proving to be much more complicated than I anticipated. Just in terms of the types of readers you get on NetGalley alone, the experience is so different. In the past, my ARC readers were people who followed me on social media, but having my book on NetGalley means total strangers are reading my book. The experience has been refreshing to hear true and unbiased opinions, but it's also been terrifying. I have a YouTube video about my experience that will be listed in the resources section for you to watch, but here's a short list of my thoughts:

- You have direct access to a massive group of readers.

- The readers know their job: review the book. They are very consistent in reviewing every book they read whether that be critically or adoringly.

- You will get a *lot* of reviews, and you won't like all of them.

- The readers read a lot of books, so they're harder to impress.

- The readers tend to have a slightly different rating scale. For example, someone can say they loved the book, but still give it three stars despite having no critiques.

- Appearing professional is a must. Don't upload an edition with typos.

- If you choose to pay by the month, you don't get to approve who can and cannot read your book. Anyone with a NetGalley account can download the book and start reading it.

- The only way to choose who can and cannot read the book is if you pay for a six-month plan.

- You get access to the emails of reviewers so you can contact them if needed.

- You are emailed every review as they come in (this is exciting at first, and anxiety-inducing as time goes on). However, you can also ask to have these emails turned off.

- This option is expensive (at least by indie author standards).

There's a lot to say about NetGalley, and I still haven't formed my true opinion on the process yet, but at the least, use my experience to weigh out the pros and cons yourself. I don't recommend debut authors using NetGalley. There's a lot of reasons for this, but mostly because getting that many opinions on your book (good and bad) can be hard as an author, especially when they're emailed to you every day. Again, please watch my YouTube video for more information on how the process went for me.

No matter how you choose to send your eBook ARC, you'll need to format your manuscript into something that can be read by e-readers such as tablets, phones, and Kindles.

How to Choose ARC Readers

Like I mentioned earlier, there are two different types of ARC readers that you'll want:

1. Readers that will write reviews on Goodreads, Amazon and other retail websites.
2. Readers that have a social media following and will share about the book online.

Option one is usually the readers that will apply to the ARC forms you share. In that case, you choose your readers based on the fact that you think they'd enjoy your book and actually write a review. Have they read and enjoyed books you've written in the past? Do they normally write reviews on Amazon? Do they normally enjoy the genre of book you're writing in? If so, they're a good fit!

If you plan on collecting ARC readers manually (aka not through StoryOrigin) then you can create a Google Form with multiple questions like these that will help you discover the answers to all these questions to make sure the reader is a good fit for your book.

For the second option, which is a reader with a social media following that you hope will feature the book on their platform, you can ask for that sort of information on your form. I prefer to reach out to influencers myself and hand-select everyone. Odds are when you reach out to people yourself, you'll get better results, but always remember when reaching out to be as professional as possible and provide the following information to anyone you want to have feature your book:

- Who you are and a link to your website.
- The book's blurb or quick elevator pitch.
- The book's cover.
- The book's release date.
- Why you reached out to them specifically.
- The benefits for them (i.e. a free copy of an awesome book!).
- And of course, your hopes that they'll be willing to leave an honest review.

You can also send a PDF sample so they can read the first few pages and see if they like it. Most importantly, use *email*! This is a pet peeve of mine. If a professional wants to partner with me in any way shape or form, email me. If someone messages me on Instagram, I will almost always say no. It's not hard to find my email, so if someone messages me on Instagram, Facebook, or Twitter, that shows a lack of effort on their part. If you looked on someone's website and can't find their email, that's when it's fine to message them on social media, but odds are there's always a way to contact them on their website.

Keep track of everyone you email. I personally

like to use either the Instagram influencer page in *The Book Launch Planner*, or an excel sheet when I start contacting a lot of people. I like to write down the date I first contacted someone. That way, if it's been a few weeks, I can know that they probably don't want to read and feature the book, and I can move on to other people. Personally, I prefer not to follow up on emails. I get so many emails every week from brands wanting to partner with me for my YouTube channel, and they follow up to ask if I saw their email. Yes, I saw the email. No, I don't want to review your random Amazon product. I just delete, delete, delete. Do you realize how much time it would take to respond to every email? And the emails they send are obviously a copy and paste email that they also sent to a few hundred other YouTubers.

That's why I don't expect replies, and why I choose not to follow up. But if you want to follow up, there's no harm done. It just might be a waste of time.

How Many ARCs to Send

It's really difficult to decide how many ARCs

you want to send out. Some authors might say the more the better, because that means more reviews on Amazon. But at the same time, the more free copies you give out, the less people there are to buy.

You could decide on how many copies to give out based on how large your platform is. If you have a small platform, maybe aim for 10-20 ARCs. Then maybe by your second book you'll have a bigger following, and you'll want to send out 20-30 ARCs. There's no right answer. You just have to pick what feels best for you and your book.

Since we're talking about giving out books for free, I'm going to touch upon an instance where you shouldn't give out books for free.

When Not to Give Out Free Books

To put it bluntly, I make my friends and family buy my books. Heck, they're the only book sales I'm guaranteed for every book I write! I know people get excited when they publish their books, and they want to give out copies to everyone, but if you give away copies to everyone who asks, who's left to buy the book?

That's not to say I don't give out any free books

though. Besides ARC readers, who gets free books from me? Friends and family *who helped* with the book writing or publishing process. And you know what? They're the ones that usually insist on buying the book because that's how much they support me. Looking back, I can count only a few times I gave a book to someone in my close circle for free, but the rest of the time everyone was eager to buy a copy, so I let them.

You will probably get many people asking for free copies of your book. They may ask because they know you, or they may ask because they just don't want to pay. Please don't give out free books unless it's for marketing purposes, or to say thank you. Giving out free books whenever asked is a bad habit that devalues your work, your time, and will get you nowhere.

For example, I used to be a hairdresser. I have my cosmetology license and I used to work in a salon. When I was in school, my instructor always told us to never do free haircuts because then everyone will want a free haircut. Well, guess what? I didn't listen and started giving out free haircuts, and I never stopped because it felt awkward to ask friends and family for money! And she was right— once you give out one free haircut, you're stuck giving free haircuts permanently. Friends talk and now everyone you know gets free haircuts. It works the same way with books. I repeat: the only time you give away free books is for marketing purposes and to say thank you to those who helped in the writing/publishing process.

Just today (literally today, as I write this), I had someone I knew in high school message me for the first time in seven years asking how I was and then… they asked if they could have a free copy of my book. And maybe it's because I've gotten bitter with age, but I ignored them.

If you ask me for a copy of my book, I will kindly tell you it's available on Amazon, or you can purchase a signed copy off my website, but otherwise I don't entertain those who want free copies. Once your book is published, ARCs are no longer a thing, therefore you should limit (or eliminate) the number of free books you hand out.

If you want give friends and family a discount, that's okay, but please do yourself a favor and charge *something*.

BONUS TIP FROM BETHANY:

Sending ARCs is always a mix of thrilling and terrifying. People are about to actually read your book! It's about to get real.

Like everything else in publishing, there's obviously a lot of options. You could send ARCs to a large group or small, or anything in-between. You could send them months in advance or right before release, or again, anything in-between. You could even choose not to send them at all—although this is one area of marketing where I'd strongly encourage you to step into it and be brave, because it's one of the most common and most successful marketing tools to this day for a reason.

Personally, I have tried a variety of things and found that my favorite method for the first book in a series or a standalone is to, first of all, send it to as many people as possible—within reason. They have to be excited about the story, of course, but I also watch for any red flags, such as a person who can't follow directions on the form. That's a good sign they just want a free book and won't bother to review, which is the entire purpose of an ARC.

When it comes to sequels in a series, I'm more picky. I ask if they've read and reviewed my other books, and I like to make sure they actually enjoyed them. If someone didn't, I wouldn't feel comfortable sending them another book, since the chances are they wouldn't like that one either.

Secondly, I like to send ARCs closer to a release than I used to. While traditional publishing starts sending ARCs months in advance, I typically wait until a month or two before release. This is partly because as indie authors, our books aren't done months before publishing like in traditional publishing, and I like to wait until the book is as close to done as possible. I will even do the proofreading step prior to sending out proof copies, although I will still include the note about it being an "Uncorrected Proof" so that readers have grace for the story if there is a typo or two that were missed.

The other reason I like to send ARCs closer to release is simply because it's easier to keep up momentum and build up hype right before release this way. If I somehow were able to finish my book six months to a year before a release and decided to do ARCs that far back, I'd be worried that by the time the release arrived, the excitement over the book would have fizzled out.

Last, but not least, no matter the size of my ARC team or how far before release they're sent out, the one thing I always do is send ARCs. Because like Mandi said, the book itself is one of the biggest promotional tools you will ever have. ARCs generate "word of mouth" promotion from other readers that will carry far more weight with their fellow readers than anything you could say as the author. Even though it might feel frustrating to some authors to give away their work for free, always remember that one free book could encourage many others to buy.

Chapter 9: Plan a Virtual Book Tour

THIS NEXT MARKETING technique can be one of the most tedious parts of planning a book launch, but also a great way to spread the word about your new release. We're going to be talking all about different types of virtual book tours that you can host for your book release! Now, I say this is the most tedious part because planning the entire thing can be a long process. With that said, I still wanted to mention it because this is something I did for my debut novel, *Essence*, and I personally believe it had a lot to do with the long-term success of the book.

Like the cover reveal tour we talked about in chapter six, you can set up a tour for yourself or you can hire a company to arrange a virtual tour for you (again, there will be a blog post by Day Leitao in the resources section with more information). While hiring out is always an option, I also wanted to go into detail on what the process will look like if you decide to arrange everything yourself. But first, let's talk about what a virtual book tour is exactly.

What is a Virtual Book Tour?

A virtual book tour is when you arrange for your book to be featured on a set number of blogs or social media accounts, such as on Instagram, YouTube, or even TikTok. During this tour, a different account or website will feature your book every day during a set period of time. Most of the time, virtual book tours last about a week, but their length can vary depending on how much planning you put into the process. Again, this is something that's actually very similar to the cover reveal tour, but this type of tour usually happens during or very close to the week of your book's release.

The goal of a virtual book tour is to be featured by a different bookish influencer/platform every day. This means you need to contact creators on the platform of your choice and ask them if they're interested in featuring your book, as well as find out what days work best for them, and how they'd like to feature your book. The following are different ideas for how your book can be featured:

- The creator posts their review of the book.
- The creator does a Q&A with you.
- You write a guest post on their blog.
- The creator hosts a giveaway for the book.
- Or maybe a mix of some of the above, such as a review plus a giveaway.

You can do all reviews, or you can get creative with the way the book will be featured and make the tour stops customized to the type of content that's normally posted on their platform. For example, if a book blogger only does book hauls with one-sentence book reviews, don't ask them to write a long book review. If a book blogger likes to feature books with pretty covers, maybe the post can highlight the cover design process for your book.

Have fun with the content on the virtual book tour and work closely with each creator. It can help make it more exciting if you make each tour stop different, meaning not every single post is a book review. For example, you could ask one person to do a book review, another to do an interview, and a third person might have you do a guest post about how you were inspired to write the story, and so on.

The idea is that people can visit the new tour stops each day without the content getting repetitive.

The tricky part is that ideally, you'll want to arrange the entire thing so that every creator participating knows what's happening every single day so they can promote it to their followers. Each post in the tour will not only promote your book, but will also say, "Want to learn more about [BOOK TITLE]? Stop by [ACCOUNT NAME] tomorrow for a [CONTENT]." This is good for your book because it will be featured on many different accounts, but it's also good for the creators because their content will get more exposure when all the creators are working together to promote each other.

How to Find Creators to Participate

Finding creators that want to participate can be harder to arrange than you may think. If I tried to arrange a virtual tour today, I'd probably have a much easier time than I did when I was arranging the tour for *Essence*. When I published *Essence,* I had no connections and knew no creators on a personal basis. Today I could arrange a week-long virtual tour relatively easily by talking to my friends, so consider who you know, but also be willing to reach out to new people.

Even if you do know creators on a personal basis who would be happy to feature your book, I like to reach out to people I don't know as well, because they're outside my circle and probably have different followers than I do. After all, the point of the virtual book tour is to have new readers discover your book.

Contact any creators that enjoy reading your genre and frequently review or talk about books. When you contact them, give them the name of the book, the book's blurb, the book cover if possible, and then let them know why you think they'd be a good match for the book and, most importantly, how being a part of the tour can benefit *them*. I like to make my emails as personal as possible. This is *not* a copy and paste email I send to multiple people. Each email is crafted for the individual person to show them I chose to email them for a reason, and that I'm someone who follows them and enjoys the content they post.

You also want to explain the blog tour, what your plans are, and what dates it will take place. End the email by asking if they'd be interested in taking part in the blog tour, and if they are, what dates they'd be available. Ideally, you'll get some responses, and you can piece together who gets what posting dates once you receive everyone's responses.

After I nail down the dates, I figure out what content will be posted. Creators will tell me what they'd like to post, and sometimes I will also guide people in a particular direction.

Contact more creators than necessary. If you need five creators for a five-day blog tour, contact closer to fifteen or twenty people. If you don't get enough responses after a week or so, contact another ten people. Keep contacting people until you fill in all the dates you need. If you contact fifteen people, and you're lucky enough that eight of them respond saying they're interested, just do an eight-day tour and take advantage of all those extra people!

If you find you're planning your blog tour and there's a day in the middle that no one can post on, this is when I'll turn to a friend to see if they'd be willing to participate in the blog tour that day to fill in the gap. If you don't have friends that are creators or have a social media platform, then you can post on that day yourself. It's not as good as having someone else post, but it's better than having a day where nothing happens.

What to Provide Creators

Like I've mentioned before, when you work with bloggers and reviewers, you want to provide them with as much information as possible. The blog tour planning process can be confusing with so many people involved, and it's your job to provide clear direction. Plus, the easier you make the process, the more likely it is that the creators will want to work with you again on future virtual tours. What you provide to creators can vary depending on the types of posts they plan to create, but the following is a good place to start:

- Book cover
- Link to the book on Amazon (and/or other vendors)
- Author bio
- Author photo
- Link to your website
- Virtual tour schedule (such as dates of the tour, the name/social media handle of each creator, what type of content they're posting, and when)

Wait to send all this information until a creator agrees to participate in the tour, otherwise you risk overwhelming them with so much information they won't want to participate.

What Should be Required of Creators?

I like to set some requirements for bloggers to make sure everyone is happy by the end of it. Besides promoting the book release, I have only one rule, and that's that I require creators to promote the tour as a whole, not just their post. This isn't for the sake of my book, it's because I want all the creators involved to have their posts featured. This means I ask each creator to tell their followers where the next day's tour stop is, and to share the entire virtual tour schedule. That way even if it's the last stop on the tour, everyone can go back and view the posts of the previous tour stops.

How to Share Information

There are many ways you can go about planning and arranging your virtual book tour. Email is the most traditional way. It can be frustrating because there's so much back and forth, but it can still be effective. When I planned everything for *Essence*, I did it all through email, and the process was stressful. I had to juggle talking to six different people and coordinate who was posting what and when. Once I had everything figured out, I created a private page on my website that had all the information about the blog tour. That page on my website contained everything the creators needed in an easy download. There was also a comment section on that website page so they could ask questions if needed.

That page of my website was password protected, and the passwords were given to all the creators participating in the virtual tour. While this process worked, in the future I may prefer to arrange everything through a Facebook group or a Discord server instead. But that also has its draw-backs because all the messaging may make the process overwhelming for the creators involved. I'm okay with feeling overwhelmed myself, but I don't want the process to feel overwhelming to my creators that are helping me promote my book. When it comes to arranging everything, go with your gut and do what you feel is best!

As you can see, the planning process can be intense, but it can be an effective tool for authors to make the most of their book release.

BONUS TIP FROM BETHANY:

In my experience, I've tried two different types of release tours: one that I set up on my own by reaching out to dozens of different Bookstagram accounts until I had enough who said yes, and the second where I worked with a Book Tour company that handled everything for me for a fee. At the time, the fee was $150 for a week of posts, plus I had to order seven books and ship each of them to the individual creators. It ended up costing roughly $250. (Note: this is not a cut and dry price, but will likely change depending on what each company offers.) These companies will have a set group of people who've specifically signed up to do tours like this, most likely with larger followings than you or I would be able to work with on our own.

While it was a weight off my shoulders to let them contact all the creators and set up the tour for me, and the larger follower numbers meant I may have reached more people than I could have if I'd contacted accounts on my own, I also had to consider ROI. Because of the extra expenses, I needed to sell roughly 100 books to make that money back (since an average royalty for an eBook is just a little over $2.50).

On the other hand, when I set up a virtual book tour on my own, I spent time instead of money. Reaching out to creators and planning everything was definitely time-consuming, but by sending eBooks only and doing all the work myself, there were zero expenses! This meant the ROI was far better, since even one book sold would lead to a profit. So if you decide to do a book release tour, it really depends on what's right for you. Sometimes it might be more beneficial to spend time, and in other cases, you might prefer to spend money and have someone else spend the time.

Chapter 10: Film and Edit a Book Trailer

BOOK TRAILERS ARE one of my favorite ways to promote my books. All of my novels have a book trailer, and the trailer for *Essence* has over 22,000 views. To me, book trailers are a fun way to promote your book and create a new medium for your story. The goal of a book trailer is to sell your book and make whoever watches the trailer want to buy the book. If the book trailer is lack-luster, it won't do the trick. If you publish a book trailer that looks unprofessional, readers may assume that the book is unprofessional as well. If you choose to do a book trailer, it's important to put in your best efforts.

There are a lot of options on how to make a book trailer, and the prices range from free to thousands of dollars. I've done just about every form of book trailer at this point, and I'll be taking the time to talk about each type of book trailer with you here.

I like to think there are three tiers of book trailers and I categorize them by price:

- Filming the trailer yourself ($)
- Using stock photos and video ($$)
- Hiring someone else to film the trailer ($$$)

Filming the Trailer Yourself

I've always loved the filming and editing process when creating my own trailers. You can make the trailer completely customized to your book. However, here are the types of things that will be on your plate if you decide to film the book trailer yourself:

- **Video scripting** - Will there be dialogue? And if not, how do you picture your trailer? Will there be actors?
- **Location scouting** - Finding a place to film

that fits your vision.

- **Casting** - If you choose to have actors, how do you picture them looking, and where will you find them?

- **Filming** - Do you have a camera? Will you be doing the filming, or will someone else film the trailer?

- **Video editing** - Do you have the skillset and software to edit the book trailer yourself?

- **Adding music/voiceover** - Where will you get the music for the trailer? Keep in mind that it needs to be royalty free.

- **Wardrobe** - If you have actors, how do they need to dress?

The process for creating a book trailer differs depending on what route you take. For example, you can choose to not have actors, and instead film locations or objects that relate to your book. Or you can bypass the filming process altogether and choose to have a completed animated book trailer, depending on what your skillset or resources are.

When I filmed the book trailer for *Essence,* we filmed in a state park near my house for some parts, while other parts were filmed on location in New Hampshire. The book was inspired by a pool of water in New Hampshire, so it was super important to me that we had clips of that included.

Before I started filming, I made a storyboard of what I wanted my shots to look like. These were just simple doodles to give me an idea of how I wanted the shots framed. I didn't do casting because I cast myself as the main character. At the end of the day the footage worked out really well! Having myself cast made my storyboard sketches especially important, since my mom was the one handling the camera and I couldn't re-frame the shots for her.

While I played the main character for my book trailer, I was also the main character on my book cover. For the shots we filmed in New Hampshire for the book trailer, we also took photos for the book cover the same day.

Because the book trailer and book cover were working together, I wore the same outfit for both. So I put a little more care into picking the wardrobe.

When it came to filming, I directed my mom on exactly what I wanted, and we spent an hour or two filming across two separate days. While the trailer is only one minute long, I probably had at at least an hour's worth of footage to sort through. We would film the same shots over and over, to make sure we had everything correct. If you watch the trailer for *Essence* (it will be linked in the resources section), you'll notice there are a lot of different shots because I really wanted to capture the overwhelming feeling of the main character, Emma, being haunted by her Essence.

I filmed the voiceover myself, and I didn't do anything fancy to accomplish this. I just talked to my camera, and then when I went into my video editing software, I removed the video portion so that all that was left was the audio.

The music for the book trailer is music I purchased the rights to. You don't have to purchase the rights to all music, but I wanted a very specific feeling for my trailer, and the only music I found that I liked was music I had to pay for the rights to use. For royalty free music that you don't have to pay for, you can find an entire library of options on YouTube. If you already have a YouTube account, then just log in and click on the YouTube Studio. On the left-hand side, you'll see the "Audio Library." Everything in that library is free to use for commercial use everywhere, not just on YouTube.

For a wider selection of royalty free music, I currently use Epidemic Sound, which is subscription based. But you can also purchase music track by track from other websites, such as Pond5. To edit everything together I use Adobe Premiere Pro, but you can also use Final Cut Pro, iMovie, or any other video editing software of your choosing.

Using Stock Photos & Video

If you don't want to use actors or film anything original, stock photos and videos are another option at your disposal. This is great if you don't have a camera to film things for yourself. There are many different video editing softwares you can use to download stock photos and/or video clips and turn them into a video to promote your book. However, it's harder to make a professional looking book trailer this way. Most often you'll see authors create book trailers using stock photos that are turned into a slide show. If you choose to use stock video/photos, it will be important to take your time editing the book trailer to make sure that the result is clean and professional.

Trailers that use stock footage are something I've done for my own books as well, such as *She's Not Here*, which is made up of stock video clips. What made the book trailer work was not the footage that was used, but how it was all edited together. Once I selected which clips worked for my book, I edited it using special transitions, text overlays, a voiceover, and flashing images. The result was an eye-catching trailer that looked professional and sold the book.

I also used stock video for my newest novel, *Meet Me at the Summit*. One of my favorite places to find good and affordable stock video is StoryBlocks, which is a monthly subscription for stock video. While you're a subscriber, you can download as much footage as you'd like, and then once you're done making your trailer, you can cancel! Using StoryBlocks, I created my book trailer for *Meet Me at the Summit* for only $50.

Hiring Someone to Film and Edit

Hiring out will usually get you the most professional results, but it can mean many different things. You can hire an amateur or maybe someone who's going to film school if you're looking for a budget-friendly option. For this example, I'm going to talk specifically about hiring a professional team with experience in the field, whose sole job is creating a book trailer.

I had the amazing experience of working with Film 14 to create a cinematic book trailer for my second novel, *I am Mercy*. Film 14 is a company that works with authors and publishers to create book trailers. Since this is the only type of video content they create, they are experts at what they do.

When you work with a company to produce a book trailer, you have the option to control almost everything, with experts there to guide you along the way. In my experience with Film 14, I provided as much information about my book as possible in a couple of pages. I let the team know what vibe I wanted the trailer to have, and I also sent along a Pinterest board I had created to show them what I was thinking in terms of visuals.

From there I worked with a team to perfect the script, finalize the wardrobe, and approve the actor they selected to play the part of my main character, Aida. I've never been one to dream about having my books made into film, but creating the book trailer with an actual actor was so fun!

After a couple of weeks, the result was a thirty-seven-second book trailer that was slightly creepy, intense, and kept you wanting more. The trailer was absolutely perfect! I have a two-part video series on YouTube where I go in-depth on the process of creating the book trailer with Film 14, so if you're ever curious, be sure to check it out! The videos will be linked in the resources section.

The biggest downside of hiring professionals is the price tag. A lot of work goes into creating a short book trailer. I worked with a producer, editor, videographer, and an actor. And of course, each person you work with needs to be paid. The cost of book trailers vary a lot, but for Film 14, their prices currently range from $500 - $15,000 depending on how high-scale the trailer is.

Return on Investment

Since we're talking about the costs of book trailers, it's very important to include a reminder about ROI, or return on investment. Book royalties vary, but let's say for the sake of easy math that your royalty per book (aka the amount of money you make per book sold) is exactly $3. That would mean that for a $3,000 book trailer, you'd need to sell at least 1,000 books to even make your money back. And that's just to pay for the book trailers—it doesn't even include all your other expenses during the publishing process, such as cover design, editors, and other marketing options!

As you can see, it's not financially savvy for indie authors to hire out for book trailers, especially since there's no way to track whether a book sale was a direct result of the book trailer. You could have a trackable link, but clicking a link doesn't always mean there was a purchase.

Traditional publishers hire out for book trailers occasionally, but they also have a much larger budget than most indie authors.

While I loved working with Film 14, and the trailer they created is my favorite book trailer out of all the book trailers I have, for the sake of full disclosure, you should know that the trailer they created for *I am Mercy* was created for free in exchange for my talking about their services on my YouTube channel. I'd always wanted to do a cinematic book trailer, and even better was given a behind the scenes look at how it was all created! But if it weren't for me promoting their service on my channel, I never would have been able to afford one of their book trailers.

This is why I love creating book trailers myself, because I can do it for free, and therefore the only return on your investment I need to worry about is my time. If you can learn to create a book trailer yourself for little to no money, you will have the best results financially.

What to Include in Your Book Trailer

No matter what type of book trailer you go with, try to emulate the type of trailers you see for movies. Leave the viewer hanging and wanting more. Make the reader see that your book has an amazing story that they just *need* to read to find out what happens next. A book trailer is more than putting your book blurb as a slideshow. It's about creating suspense and giving readers a reason to buy your book. Here are some things to consider having featured in your trailer:

- Book cover.
- Release date.

- Where they can buy.
- Author website.
- Genre of the book.
- Quote from a book review.
- A condensed version of the book's blurb.

When to Post Your Book Trailer

There's no rule for when you should post your book trailer. I think it will vary depending on your book launch plan and the book itself. In the past, I've always posted book trailers before the book was published as a way of building up excitement and promoting the pre-order. When I worked with Film 14 to create the new book trailer for *I am Mercy*, the trailer was posted years after the book was published and was a way of breathing new life into an older book.

For *Meet Me at the Summit*, I posted the book trailer on release day as a celebration of the book being released. I like to think there's no bad time to post and promote your book trailer. However, make sure that if you post a book trailer, you're using it to promote sales. Don't post the trailer until you at least have your pre-order link ready so you can take full advantage of this.

When to Skip a Book Trailer

As much as I love book trailers, I want to stress that you don't *need* a book trailer. Trailers can be a fun and effective marketing tool, but it will not make or break your marketing plan. I think a lot of authors want to create a book trailer because it's a tangible way to bring your book to life in a very similar way to book cover design. But book trailers aren't for everyone. Perhaps you don't know the first thing about planning a book trailer, or you're uninspired, or maybe you don't know how to edit videos and don't have the budget to hire out. Book trailers are nice to have, but they are not necessary. Could they help sell your book? Yes. Can you still sell books without a trailer? Yes!

I invite you to experiment with creating a book trailer, but please only do it if you truly want to, not because you feel obligated to as a part of the publishing process.

BONUS TIP FROM BETHANY:

Book trailers are one of the least necessary and

least common marketing options on our list—you absolutely do not need to feel pressured to do one! But if you have the time and willingness to figure them out, they are definitely a lot of fun for both you and your readers! I have to agree with Mandi about the costs though. With other marketing tools, you can often track your return on investment and see how many book sales that particular marketing strategy made for you, but with book trailers, it can be difficult to pinpoint if the sale came from the trailer or from other marketing. In my experience, a trailer is going to be the most exciting to readers who were already planning to buy the book anyway, but it is less effective for reaching new readers who've never heard of the book before.

My favorite style of video editing is to use still shots or video, whether the book cover, graphics that I made, or in some cases, pictures that I took myself. I also have a tutorial on how to create your own book trailer using iMovie specifically, which we will include in the resources section.

As far as the best time to publish a book trailer, while I agree with Mandi that a trailer can be fantastic marketing at any time, I personally love utilizing a book trailer as part of my cover reveal.

This can make revealing the cover itself especially exciting for readers.

Chapter 11: Release Day Marketing & Celebrations!

YOUR BOOK'S RELEASE day can be extremely stressful, fun, relaxing, or all of the above. Most of all, it's a huge marketing opportunity, because it's going to be the day where you'll most likely have the most purchases and free publicity because people are posting about the book online.

The day your book is released can be strange because you technically don't have to do anything. Your eBook is scheduled to be published in advance, and you should have submitted your print book for publication a few days ahead of time. This means on release day, you have nothing you're *required* to do. Odds are, the handful of days leading up to release will actually be the most stressful ones. You're going to rush to make sure that your files have been accepted, that your newsletter is scheduled to go out, and that you have a plan for what you want to post on social media on release day. You may reach release day and think, "Wow, what am I supposed to do now?" Or you could potentially spend release day freaking out because of a tech issue or other unexpected problem. That happens a lot too.

It's hard to anticipate what issues may arise on release day, but I highly suggest submitting your paperback book extra early so you know things will go smoothly. An error message from your print on demand company is not a good way to spend release day, or the days leading up to release.

Most of the time you'll spend the day of release online, posting about the book on social media and re-sharing things that other people post as they buy your book. That's the ideal situation. To make things even more exciting, you can also host a few different types of events on release day, such as:

- Facebook release party
- Livestream release party
- In-person release party

Facebook Release Party

A Facebook release party is a virtual event you host through Facebook events. You, as well as other authors, post about your book that's releasing, and the participating authors of the event also get the chance to promote their own books. Think of it as a virtual book fair. For the release of *I am Mercy,* I did a virtual release event and got a handful of other authors involved as well. As the host of the release party, you would post the first and last hour of the day, and then every other hour a different author takes over. During their allotted hour, participating authors can post about their book, but they will also shout out *your* book at the beginning and end of their hour. Each author will post every ten-or-fifteen minutes during their hour, and they can share all kinds of things that might entice readers, such as games, giveaways, livestreams, quizzes, or anything else to do with the books. This makes it a win-win-

win for everyone. First, because all the authors involved are able to promote their book, as well as your book. Second, because all of you reach brand new readers by combining audiences. And third, because readers are more than happy to attend for a chance to win giveaways, discover new books, and enjoy the other activities.

These release parties can be stressful to plan because of working with multiple other authors, but they're effective! Each author that participates tells their followers to come to the Facebook release party, so you often end up with a lot of readers participating in the event, including readers who have never heard of you or your books before.

The release party for *I am Mercy* had eight other authors hosting, which meant the event lasted ten hours (I hosted the first and last hour). If you're interested in learning more, the Facebook event is still available to scroll through in case you want an idea of what the posts look like, and you can refer to the resource section of this book for the link.

Livestream Party

If you're someone who's on social media a lot,

a livestream party could be the best way to connect with your readers in real time. I've done many live release parties, whether they were for my own books, or it was a livestream to join an author friend who was releasing their book. I always host my livestreams on YouTube because that's my main platform, but you can host livestreams in so many places now, so host wherever your main audience is and where you're most comfortable.

There are so many options for what you can do during the livestream. The sky's the limit, but here are some of my favorite activities:

- Answer questions from readers.
- Read a chapter from the book.
- Talk about the behind the scenes of creating the book.
- Share fun reveals.
- Play games (book-themed or just fun ice-breakers).
- Bring on friends to join you and discuss the book together.

Try to brainstorm your own ideas as well and see what you can come up with! Even better, see if you can come up with activities that have to do with your book! I like to make the livestream as fun as possible and invite friends to join me and play games. The most recent release day livestream I participated in was Bethany's release party for *The Enchanted Crown,* and it was such a blast! A link to the livestream replay will be available at the back of the book for livestream inspiration.

In-Person Release Party

A personal favorite of mine is having an in-person release party! There are a few different ways you can host your own release party, but I'd say the two major options are: (1) to have a release party at a bookstore, or (2) to host a party at a location of your choosing. And that location could be your house, a local park, or anywhere you want to host an event!

In chapter twelve, I'll be going into detail about how you can host events like bookstore signings, self-hosted events, and selling your books at vendor fairs. For now I want you to remember one thing:

Tell Everyone About Your Book!

Your number one goal on release day, besides making sure your book is live on vendor websites, is telling everyone it's available for purchase. And by tell everyone, I mean post on social media, update Goodreads, send your newsletter, and announce it anywhere else you can think of. Release day is your day to post as much as you want about your book.

If you'd like, there's a page in *The Book Launch Planner* with a complete to-do list of things you can do on release day to make sure you cover all your bases. At this point, you may have a few book reviews on Goodreads, but Amazon and other vendors don't allow reviews until the book is published. This means release day is also the day you can start asking for book reviews on vendor websites.

Most importantly, make sure you leave time to celebrate! You not only wrote a book, but you published the book! And that's an entire feat within itself. Take the next few days to relax and soak in the glory of seeing readers enjoy the story you've worked so hard to create.

BONUS TIP FROM BETHANY:

I'm guessing it's obvious at this point that I like to try different options when it comes to marketing, so I've experimented with going all out on the day of a book release:

- Sending out a newsletter.
- Emailing my ARC team to review.
- Posting multiple times on social media.
- Reposting everyone's excitement.
- Spending hours responding with personalized thank you messages.
- Putting together a huge livestream release event with friends.

On the other hand, I've also done a quiet, simple release:

- Newsletter was scheduled in advance.
- Posted once on social media (and of course still reposted and thanked everyone for sharing).

Otherwise, I spent a very quiet day at home and celebrated by watching Netflix with ice cream. And of course, my releases have been a wide range of everything in-between.

While planning out an official celebration is

without a doubt more work and more stress, I'd have to say those events—or even just going out to a special meal at the end of the day to celebrate—have always made my release day feel more special, because I'm able to share my excitement with others. Inviting your readers and/or author friends to celebrate with you turns a solo experience into something you can share together. Even though I am a high introvert who gets extremely anxious about events with other people (like many writers!), I have always been thankful that I stepped outside of my comfort zone in this area and will always treasure those moments with friends, family, and fans.

If you feel strongly that it's not for you, don't worry about it. Everyone is different! But if you're on the fence and are considering it, then I'd encourage you to do some research and look into your options. Maybe there is a more low-key possibility, or people you trust who could help you. If you're able and willing, you could even practice— whether that means practicing making food in advance for an in-person party, or hosting a livestream with someone else prior to release day, or whatever else. This could help you feel more comfortable on the big day as well. No matter what you choose to do, I agree with Mandi—enjoy that day to the fullest!

But also make sure the marketing doesn't stop on release day. It's so common to see an author spend months or years pouring their time, money, and heart into their book—only to stop talking about it right after release day. In fact, sometimes, out of pure exhaustion I've done this for a bit myself. But like Mandi has laid out in this chapter, you didn't do all that work just to forget about it and move on! We want to encourage you to not stop talking about your book. Don't be afraid to keep mentioning it from time to time. Whether on social media, or your newsletter, or another platform, there's a good chance that the most recent time you mention your book will be the very first time someone has ever heard about it. Even if you personally feel like you've talked about it a thousand times, it will still be fresh to someone. But of course, you can also talk about it in a way that's fresh for you and your current readers too.

One of the best pieces of advice I ever received was to make sure you're splitting your marketing focus between (1) your current readers, getting them excited for what you have coming next, and also (2) brand new readers, and introducing them to the books you already have out. This balance can help you feel more comfortable bringing up your book after it's published, when you think of all the new readers who haven't heard about it yet and are going to love it!

Chapter 12: Sell Books at Events on Release Day & After

MANY AUTHORS MAY not have the same mindset as me, but my all time favorite way to sell my books is at events. You can do an event to celebrate a book release, or at any time after your book is published to help promote the book! At this point, I feel like I've done every type of book event under the sun. I've done conventions, bookstore signings, vendor fairs, farmers markets, self-hosted events, and expos. All these events I've done in the past can be broken down into three categories: bookstore events, self-hosted events, and vendor fair events. And these are exactly what I'll be talking about in this chapter!

We'll be going over how to find and arrange these types of events, how selling your book will work, and how to make the most of each event to get your book out to more readers!

Bookstore Events

The dream of many authors is to see their book on the shelf of their favorite local bookstore. Or, even better, signing copies of books at that bookstore! To arrange a book signing at a bookstore, usually the best approach is to contact a bookstore and talk to them about allowing you to host an event there.

Working with bookstores can sometimes be a little complicated because you have to figure out payments for the books, but if your dream is to sell your book in stores, go for it! You can also ask to leave a couple signed copies behind for the store to sell later on. Barnes and Noble is now starting to work with indie authors to sell copies of their books, but policies may vary from location to location. Barnes and Noble will sometimes consider buying your book through Ingramspark (if you published through them), because this company allows bookstores to return unsold copies by mailing them back to you. This makes book purchases less risky for the bookstore.

Indie bookstores usually work slightly differently. They will sometimes buy the books through a distributor just like Barnes & Noble, but I've found most of the time indie bookstores like to buy their stock directly from indie authors and create a consignment contract. Selling your book on consignment means you get paid *after* the book is sold. A contract is created between the store and the author deciding what dates the book needs to be sold by, how much the bookstore makes, and when you're required to pick up unsold books.

When I have my books on consignment, I like to keep a record of everything and set reminders for myself when the books need to be sold. That way I can follow up with the bookstore. Most of the time the bookstore will contact you if they need to return the book, but keeping track of where your books are in stock helps to make sure nothing ever falls through the cracks. There was a time that I accidentally had my books on consignment for over a year because I had forgotten about it and so did the bookstore. When you do sell a book through consignment, the store will contact you to pick up a check for the books sold, or they'll mail it directly to you!

Self-Hosted Events

Let's say release day for your book is coming up and you want to have a party where you can sell copies of your book, but you don't want it to be as formal as a book signing where people come to the store to buy your book and leave. Let's say you'd rather people stick around to celebrate with you!

In this case, it may be the most fun to do a self-hosted event, whether that be at your house, in a park, or in a building you rent out for the day. I've done self-hosted release parties for two of my novels, *Essence* and *She's Not Here*. The release party for *Essence* was hosted at my parents' house, and we told people a window of time I'd be signing books. The result was a constant stream of people coming and going the entire day. By the end of the signing, I sold over eighty copies of my book. We also had snacks for people to help them stick around a little longer and celebrate.

In my opinion, the best part of self-hosted events where you sell copies of your book, is that you don't have to share the money with anyone. You get to keep all the profit, rather than letting the bookstore get a cut. Now, of course, in this case you'll have to handle the sales yourself, but I found that at events like this most people bring cash to buy the book.

I know a lot of people will think, "Well, what about the people that don't know me personally and want to come to the event? I don't want to invite strangers to my house."

If I'm being 100% honest with you, I will let you know that when you release your first book and you don't have a large platform, the only people coming to a book signing specifically to buy your book are people who know you personally. It's fun to think strangers who just happen to be shopping in a bookstore will see you signing books and feel inclined to buy it, but that's not very common. I've done many book signings at stores, and the only time strangers came to the signing intentionally was when it was a large event that the store put on. This meant that there were many authors signing in one day, which naturally attracted a larger crowd. That's not to say a book signing at a store is a bad idea, because it's not! Again, for some authors it's a dream to have a signing in a favorite bookstore, and your friends and family can come to support you and make it a fantastic day. But you can also do this in your own home, where a bookstore won't take a cut of your sales.

When it comes to trying to decide where you want to have your release party it breaks down to what your goals are and what your motivation behind having the signing is.

When to Have a Book Signing in a Bookstore

- If you want to have a traditional book signing.
- If you want to invite people to the book signing who you aren't comfortable giving your home address to.
- If you don't want to worry about how to handle the transaction of selling the book.
- If you want to leave signed copies of your book at the store when you leave (although not all stores do this, and you will have to ask what each

bookstore's policy is).

- If you want to live out your dream of seeing copies of your book for sale in a bookstore.

When to Have a Book Signing at Your Home:

- If you're comfortable with giving everyone your home address.
- If you're comfortable handling transactions, although it's okay if you tell people you can only accept cash.
- If you want a signing where you can sell your book and have fun with the people you invite (for example, with a cookout, yard games, etc.).
- If you want to make more money per book sale.

If you choose to host a release party yourself, you can always do a more traditional book signing later on down the line. You can have a book signing at any time. Take it from someone who does book signings at least once a month. I don't have signings at bookstores very often anymore, but I'm constantly doing book signings at vendor fairs and conventions. It's become a great source of income, as well as exposure. Speaking of which, let's discuss vendor fairs next!

Vendor Fair Events

I've been doing vendor fair events for a couple of years now, and in the past couple of months I feel like I've figured out what works for me and what doesn't. Now, I should point out, selling at vendor fairs—or any event—is a step you can skip as an author, but I've found it to be a huge way to continue to sell books years after the book has been published.

If you're an introvert, then the thought of selling your book at vendor fairs may sound like torture, but if you're like me and you tend to be more extroverted and love everything about vendor fairs—including shopping—this may be right up your alley!

How to Find Vendor Fairs

I tend to do vendor fairs about once a month, so usually the first question I get from fellow authors is, "How do you find vendor fair events?" When I first started doing events, it was extremely hard to find any, never mind finding vendor events that had large crowds in attendance. Even worse, the vendor events

I did find had huge table fees that made it almost impossible to break even. For example, when I went searching for vendor events on Google, I'd find events that were two hours away and cost $200+ to have booth space.

The key to finding good vendor events is to find Facebook event listings. Facebook has been the #1 reason I've found vendor fair events to apply to this year. Usually if I see a Facebook friend post that they're going to an event, I check out that event and see if they're still looking for vendors. The events that tend to catch my eyes are farmers markets, local vendor fairs, strawberry festivals, and fall festivals. Depending on where you live, your local area will usually have events like this, and the town will make a Facebook event to advertise. When you find the Facebook event, visit the event's website to see if they're accepting vendors, and fill out their application.

I've found once you discover one vendor fair, it's much easier to find more. When I'm at vendor fairs, I like to talk to the other vendors in attendance and ask them what their favorite vendor fairs are. Even better, I like to add the other vendors as friends on Facebook. This is because they will usually post about other events that they'll be attending and I can use that as an opportunity to apply to that event.

The more events you go to, the more events you'll discover. Soon enough, you'll have a long list of events you can attend every year. The real trick is figuring out which ones are worth your time and money, which brings us to our next point.

Which Events to Attend & How Much Should You Pay?

Vendor fairs will almost always have a booth/table fee. This is the fee you have to pay to be a part of the event, and it can vary. Prices can range anywhere from free to $2000+, and I've had experience with a wide range.

Sometimes, vendor fairs will also ask that you donate one of your products to be used as a raffle prize, which is something you should factor into the price of the event when you're considering it.

I've only experienced one vendor fair that was free, and that was a vendor fair I did at a local campground. The campground had an application that vendors could fill out, and they invited their favorites to the campground for a special event. This was a win for the campground because it was a fun event for all the campers to enjoy, and it's a win for the vendors because we could sell our products without paying a fee.

Free events, however, are very rare. Most times you'll find events in the $75-$150 range, and I've found that's my sweet spot in terms of the price I'm willing to pay. An event priced in that range is usually cheap enough that there's low risk on my end, but the event is established enough that there will be enough foot traffic to make money.

The larger the event is, the more expensive booth space will be. For example, my booth at BookCon was almost $2000 (which was split between myself and my co-author Bethany Atazadeh). Smaller events, like local Comic Cons, tend to be $100-$400.

When it comes to choosing which events you go to, it's important to think about what type of audience will be there. General vendor fairs can be a hit or miss for some authors, but for me personally, they're usually a huge hit because I write in so many genres and can therefore cater to a larger audience. On the other hand, authors who write in mainly fantasy will have greater success at Comic Con events because the audience there is mainly there for those fantasy elements.

Different books will sell better at different events. For example, one of my best events to date has been a chocolate and wine festival. The best seller at that event was *She's Not Here*, a psychological thriller novel. This genre was a perfect match for the type of person that loves to curl up with a glass of wine and read a book that's on the darker side. At FanExpo Boston, my best seller was *I am Mercy*, which is a historical fantasy novel that involves dark magic and witchcraft, and is a perfect match for Comic Cons.

It may take you a while to find events that go well with the type of books that you write, but once you do, you'll notice an increase in sales!

Vendor Booth Displays

Perhaps the hardest part of preparing for a vendor fair is figuring out your booth display. How your booth looks can make or break a sale. If your booth is plain, you may not even have the opportunity to pitch your book to attendees, because they won't notice it. So it's important to create a set-up that is beautiful, professional, and eye-catching.

There are endless possibilities for creating a booth display, and your biggest inspiration will be other vendors. Go to farmers markets and fairs, and see how their booths are set up. Take note of what's catching your eye. Do you like when booths have shelving, signs, and/or colorful decorations?

My booth has changed a lot over the years. I started with just a table where I propped up my books, but now I have two shelves and folding signs.

My main bookshelf sits in front of my table and displays most of my book stock. This bookshelf was purchased from Amazon, and the shelves pop out so that the shelf can fold up and fit into my car for easy transport. The second shelf sits on my table and also folds up, but it was made by my husband who built two shelves like this for me.

Booth set up for a vendor fair

Besides shelving, I also have plenty of signs to promote what I'm selling and what the prices are. My display is constantly changing as I release new books and add new products to my display. Besides books, I also sell stickers and enamel pins, all of which are on display to show customers that walk by what they can purchase.

How to Set Up & Break Down Your Booth

Every vendor fair will have a load in and out time for your booth. This is the allotted time you have to set up and take down your booth before and after the event, and the faster you can do it, the better. When I'm by myself, I can usually get my booth set up within an hour. This is because it usually only takes me two trips to unload everything from the car. One trip is for my table and canopy tent (which I only use if the event is outside), and the second trip is for everything else. I'm able to limit my trips because I have a large dolly that allows me to pile on all my books and my shelf displays, and wheel everything over all at once. When it comes to a dolly or cart, in my opinion, the bigger the better! My large dolly is the only one I use now, and it can also fold up for easy transport.

How to Collect Money

The thing that confuses people the most is how to collect money at vendor fairs, but it's much easier than you would think! The first option is cash, which is pretty straightforward. All you need is to make sure you can make change. The second option is to take debit/credit cards. To take cards, you'll need to sign up for some sort of card reader like Square or Clover. I've also seen vendors that accept payment over Venmo or PayPal, but customers need to have a Venmo or PayPal account in order to use that option.

For my business, I use the Square App. It's free to sign up, and they just take a small percentage of each sale you make. If you'd like, you can even get by without purchasing the card reader that attaches to your phone and enter the cards manually instead, but I recommend getting a card reader to make the process faster.

To get a card reader, you can purchase one through their website. Sometimes they even do promotions where you can get the reader free just by signing up. Once you get the app and card reader, you simply plug it into your phone, open the app, and swipe to accept payments.

I only have experience with the Square reader, but I love it. I especially like the option to add my books and products under the "Items" section, so that when someone wants to buy a book, I just tap on the book they want and it adds in the price automatically. This also means at the end of the event I can create a report to see how many books I sold, and which ones I sold the most of. Using the Square App also lets me keep track of sales tax, which is often what keeps people from wanting to do vendor fairs.

Sales Tax ID & Reporting Sales Tax

Figuring out sales tax is the most confusing part of the equation, but I'm going to try to break it down as much as possible. Full disclaimer: I'm not a tax professional. For full advice, please speak to an accountant.

Before you can sell at events, you'll need a sales tax ID, and you'll need a different ID for each state you sell in. If you do an event in New York, you need a New York sales tax ID. If you do an event in Connecticut, you'll need a sales tax ID for Connecticut. Larger events will sometimes ask for your sales tax ID before they'll accept you into the event. This is because some vendor fairs report which businesses attend events to the state, and therefore can see if you fail to report sales tax.

Getting a sales tax ID varies from state to state, so please look up the process for where you're planning on selling your items. To apply you'll need to visit your state's government website.

Let's talk about reporting sales tax next. Each state will have a different sales tax percentage. To learn what the percentage is in the state where you are selling, you'll need to visit your state's government website, or do a simple Google search. To charge sales tax, you can do so using the Square App (or whichever credit card service you choose), by going into the settings and entering the sales tax percentage. Once you've done that, sales tax will automatically be added during the checkout process. At the end of each event, you can create a report to see how much sales tax you owe the state.

Sometimes states have different requirements for reporting sales tax. The method for reporting varies from state to state, and also by country, so please look into the requirements for where you live and sell books.

What Are You Selling?

Now that you know what the selling process is, let's talk about what you're selling. Obviously you're going to be selling your books, but you don't need to be limited to just your books. My booth has grown a lot over the years—from just to books, to books, stickers, and pins. I like to consider myself a mini-stationary store. While books will be your priority, feel free to sell other items you create (or have created) that go along with your books or are a part of your business. Here are other items you could sell:

- Signed books
- Stickers
- Pins
- Magnets
- Handmade bookmarks (not just the paper ones people can get for free)
- Character art (if you have permission from the artist)

The possibilities are endless! Just keep in mind that if you're selling items with art on them, that you need to own the rights to that art.

How to Price Your Items

Pricing your book for vendor fairs tends to be slightly different than how you'd price them for retail websites. My paperback novels are normally $12.99, but for vendor fairs, they're $15. I price them higher for two reasons:

1. The book is signed, therefore more valuable.

2. I want to be able to encourage the sale of multiple books. I set it up so that the more books someone buys, the cheaper it is per book. If you buy two books, you save $5. If you buy three books, you save $10. You get the idea. In order to do a sale like this, I need to give the book a slightly higher price than usual, so I can still make a profit.

I always like to have a nice, round number for the price as well, this way if someone pays cash, it's easy to make change. While I always carry plenty of dollar bills on me, I very rarely have small change.

What to Bring to Events

I like to think that I have packing for events down to a science, but the truth is, I have a closet in my house dedicated to vendor fairs and keep everything there in one place so I never have to think much about it. While what you need may vary from event to event, here's my basic list of items you could consider bringing:

- Table.
- Chair.

- Canopy tent (if the event is outside).
- Cash box (with plenty of change).
- Debit/credit card reader.
- Small sign saying you take debit/credit card.
- Sign that says the price of your items.
- Sharpie (to sign your books).
- Tape & scissors (you don't always need them, but I've found it's useful to have them on hand).
- Table cloth.
- A large, fun sign saying what you sell.
- Stock of your books/items you're selling.
- Business cards.
- Shelving/other items you can use to display your books.
- A dolly/cart to transport everything to and from your car.
- Food/snacks (you may not be able to leave your booth to eat).
- Proof of tax ID (not always required, but sometimes they ask you to bring it).

Vendor fairs can be a blast, though preparing for your first one may feel overwhelming. I went into my first events without any prior knowledge and slowly learned as I went. As you get more familiar with the process, you'll sell more and more books! If you'd like a closer look behind the scenes, check out the resources sections where there will be videos I've posted on my YouTube channel talking about my experience with specific events.

BONUS TIP FROM BETHANY:

I've done a few events like these as well, such as BookCon, the Twin Cities Book Festival, multiple signings at Barnes & Noble, a couple library book signings, and other smaller events. As a high introvert, I can tell you it's stressful but worth it! Being prepared with everything Mandi mentioned will help take some of the anxiety away, but a few other things that help me are:

1. Bringing and/or inviting friends to come, because it helps to see a friendly face!

2. Planning a "reward" of some type that you can look forward to after the event is done, such as a fancy coffee drink to treat yourself!

3. Writing down some quick one-liner ideas for telling strangers about your book, so you don't have to come up with things on the spot.

4. Also writing down some quotes or notes to yourself for how you want to sign your books.

5. And then hype yourself up about being excited to talk to people and get as ready as you can!

These things have helped me feel more confident during an event, but I think my favorite advice is to make the most of it. It only lasts a few hours, and then you'll never see most of these people again. So stand up, make eye contact, wave, say hi, and make an effort to talk to those passing by your booth or table. This will make a world of difference in both your sales and in your having a wonderfully exhausting, positive experience!

Chapter 13:
Marketing
Post-Release

AFTER YOU PUBLISH a book there's always a sense of, "Well, now what?" For months you've been living deadline by deadline, and now all of the sudden there's nothing left on your to-do list—until you publish another book, when you get to start the publishing process all over again.

Once your book is out, you could technically choose to never promote it again, but if you want to make sales long after the release, your work isn't done.

Your book won't keep up the same level of sales forever, and over time the sales will naturally dip. Even if you do all the right things to set your book up for success—gorgeous cover, stong description, well-researched keywords—at the end of the day, the best thing you can do is to continually talk about your book. Marketing is all about coming up with new, creative ways to promote your book using all the methods we've talked about in this book series.

Continue to Get Book Reviews

After your book is released, your goal is to get as many book reviews as possible on retail websites—especially Amazon, since that's where most indie author sales come from. At this point, you should have already reached out to your street team and advanced readers to ask them to write a review, but you also need to post about it on social media. Educate your friends and family who have read the book on the importance of book reviews, and how the more reviews a book has, the more willing readers will be to buy a book because it creates a level of trust in the author.

There's a few different things you can do to encourage book reviews:

- Feature reviews on social media.

- Post occasionally on social media asking for reviews.

- Ask your newsletter subscribers to consider reviewing if they've read the book.

- If someone on social media says they read the book and loved it, respond to the comment by thanking them for reading and saying you hope they'll leave a review on Amazon.

To Look at Reviews, or Not to Look? That's the Question!

This is also the time where I have to point out that reviews are for readers, not for authors. It's easy to take bad reviews personally because your book is your baby. But not everyone is going to love your book. In fact, I like to think that once you get your first one-star review it means you've reached a wider audience. If you only get five-star reviews, it means the only people writing reviews are friends and family. But a one-star review means strangers are reading your book, and that's a good thing!

I hate looking at the reviews for my books. Even scrolling through the four and five-star reviews makes me nervous that hidden within a glowing review, there might be one sentence that will make me regret reading it.

The purpose of book reviews is to allow new readers to decide whether or not the book will be a good fit for them. Reviews are not meant to bash authors or give authors a pat on the back. Reviews are just a way of allowing the public to rate the book and help others decide if it's worth their time before they buy.

I would suggest that you don't read your reviews. Instead, have a friend sort through the reviews for you. They can copy and paste the good reviews into a document that you can reference whenever you want to use a review to promote the book.

There are rare exceptions to this where I will look through more critical reviews of my book to learn what I did wrong and see how I can improve as a writer on future books. However, it's not something I do often. And when I do, I go in reminding myself that a review is just one person's opinion and doesn't make or break my book.

Simple Ways to Promote on Social Media

There are so many little ways you can promote your book on social media. So many that we have an entire book on this topic in the Marketing for Authors Series, called *Secrets to Selling Books on Social Media*. I definitely recommend checking out that book, but until then I'm happy to give you a quick list of ideas for how you can continue to market your book on social media long after release day.

A lot of the time, the best way to promote your book on social media is to follow trends. For example, as I write this, TikTok is becoming huge and helping books blow up. If there's a fun way to use a popular sound (aka the audio options you can include in your video) to promote your book, go for it! That's a great way to market. It can also be the hardest way to market, because trends are constantly changing and you usually have to be the first to jump on something in order for it to be effective.

The following is a list of ideas for what you can

post on social media to promote your book, and you can modify these ideas to fit different platforms and trends:

- Behind the scenes of how you wrote your book.
- Inspiration behind your book.
- Quotes from the book.
- Feature characters from the book.
- Feature locations from the book.
- Talk about why you wrote the book.
- Answer commonly asked questions about the book.

My favorite way to come up with promotion ideas is to watch other creators and how they hop on new trends. The creators I look to for inspiration aren't always other authors either. Sometimes they're business owners, travelers, or gamers. How they market themselves can give me ideas on how to creatively market my own work.

How to Keep Book Sales Coming In

On paper, continuing to get book sales is simple:

- Consistently post on an online platform.

- Run ads for your book (whether Facebook, Amazon, BookBub, etc.).

- Run sales (whether a discount or even making the book temporarily free).

- Get creators to feature your book (continuing those virtual book tours we talked about in chapter nine).

- Continue to collect book reviews on vendor websites.

- Host book signing events.

- And numerous other marketing techniques.

It's simple enough to talk about all these things, but it's an entirely different task to actually do all of them. You'll likely want to do everything at once, but the reality is that you have to pick and choose marketing techniques to avoid overextending yourself and find what works for you. However, no matter what you choose, it's important to choose something that you can continue to do consistently. Book marketing isn't something you do for a few days or a few months, and then you're done. You're going to be constantly learning and growing.

In the same way you used a timeline to plan your pre-release marketing, you may find it beneficial to also create a post-release marketing calendar for yourself. This will help you have a broad overview of what you're doing to market your book and keep sales coming in.

The best advice I can give you to sell more books is to multitask less and focus on individual tasks more. What I mean by this is don't read a book on marketing (like this one) and assume you have to do it all, all at once. Overwhelming yourself with more tasks than you can handle just ends in burnout and very little book sales. Instead, put your efforts into a manageable list of marketing tactics that you think will work for you.

The Ever-Changing Marketing Landscape

The final piece of advice I want to give you is to be prepared to pivot. Marketing is constantly changing. To keep your head above water, you need to be prepared for change. In my career as an author and a business owner, I've learned about a little thing called growing pains. For a long time, I was doing the same thing and it was working. Then one day, the thing I was doing to market my books wasn't working anymore. I needed to pivot my efforts. This process of changing how you work and learning new skills is uncomfortable, but the outcome is book sales that grow exponentially.

Be careful of getting stuck in a routine when it comes to marketing. You may find that when you're doing the same thing every day, eventually you stop making sales. Constantly seek to learn and be inspired, and I promise you the results will be worth it.

Thanks for reading!

We hope that you've gained invaluable information, motivation, and encouragement from this book about making your book launch as successful as it can possibly be.

If you'd like to get to know us more, read our other books, or browse the free learning opportunities we've included for you, please check out the last two chapters. You'll find a ton of valuable information and resources to help you further.

Read the Entire Marketing for Authors Series:

As you know, this is a series of books focused on marketing techniques for authors.

Book 1, *How Your Book Sells Itself,* is about ten different aspects of your book that can make or break book sales all by itself, and how to improve your book details to enhance sales.

Book 2, *Grow Your Author Platform*, is about building up a well-rounded platform where readers can find you, including your website, your author newsletter, your content marketing, and more.

Book 3, *Book Sales That Multiply,* is about paid advertising, whether on a platform like Facebook, Amazon, Instagram, Goodreads, or even email advertisements.

Book 4, *Secrets to Selling Books on Social Media*, is focused on how to sell your book organically on social media, no matter what platform, and increase your sales.

And lastly, book 5, *Plan a Profitable Book Launch*, which you've just finished reading!

Feel free to tag us on social media!

We're so excited to see what you do with the information in this book. If you decide to make any changes based on the advice here and you're comfortable sharing and tagging us on social media, please do! We'd love to hear about your book and your success story!

Thank you again for reading!
Sincerely, Bethany & Mandi

Resources

Chapter 1 (One Million & Two Things to To):

- Hiring a Book Editor – Book Editing Costs & Where to Find Your Editor For Your Self-Published Book (Mandi Lynn):

  https://www.youtube.com/watch?v=E82X9kMH9yQ&t=1s

- How I Edit My Novel Using an Editorial Assessment Letter & Picking Beta Readers (Mandi Lynn):

  https://www.youtube.com/watch?v=pCrlKqBiBEw&t=674s

- How to Work With a Book Cover Designer (Mandi Lynn):

  https://www.youtube.com/watch?v=XU2h0NOQvYQ&t=1s

- Book Cover Design That Sells (Mandi Lynn):

https://www.youtube.com/watch?v=gPrC
R6ePs8M&t=1s

- How To Format a Novel in Microsoft Word - Self-Publishing (Mandi Lynn):
  https://www.youtube.com/watch?v=2042
  28daXU4&t=177s
- How to Format an eBook & Send Free Copies for Kindle (Mandi Lynn):
  https://www.youtube.com/watch?v=yU5
  MqK4erXc
- Book Formatting with InDesign & How to Do Paperback Pre-Orders on IngramSpark (Mandi Lynn):
  https://www.youtube.com/watch?v=6ed
  M19RZ2i8&t=206s
- Planning My Book Launch – Children's Book Release Plan (Mandi Lynn): https://
  www.youtube.com/watch?v=0bj
  kQipOis
- Planning a Book Release (Bethany Atazadeh):
  https://youtu.be/mGQZQB-aZms
- How to Do a Book Release (Bethany

Atazadeh):

https://youtu.be/SDzWsOVhLZs

- My Top 3 Tips for a Book Release (Bethany Atazadeh):

  https://youtu.be/yWuTdnNUjCg

Chapter 2 (Start Marketing Yesterday):

- Goodreads Librarian Group:

  https://www.goodreads.com/group/show/220-goodreads-librarians-group

Chapter 4 (Create a Publishing & Marketing Timeline):

- The Book Launch Planner:

  https://stoneridgebooks.com/the-book-launch-planner/

- Gantt Chart Publishing Timeline Download:

  https://exciting-engineer-5402.ck.page/858773295e

- Plan a Successful Book Launch - Book Release Template:

  https://www.youtube.com/watch?v=ovb6L4mnQcM&t=3s

Chapter 5 (Are Pre-Orders an Effective Marketing Strategy?):

- The Courtney Project, What it Takes to Become a USA Today Bestseller:

  https://www.youtube.com/watch?v=MuQJU-SMUuA&t=415s

- The Courtney Project, USA Today Bestseller List:

  https://www.youtube.com/watch?v=Y_oBWVhwCIs

- Setting Up eBook Pre-Orders on Amazon + Pre-Order Campaign Incentives to Sell More Books (Mandi Lynn):

  https://www.youtube.com/watch?v=1L2TUHJgOIQ&t=642s

- Book Formatting with InDesign & How to Do Paperback Pre-Orders on IngramSpark (Mandi Lynn):

  https://www.youtube.com/watch?v=6edM19RZ2i8&t=222s

- Increase Pre-Order Book Sales +paperback pre-orders (Mandi Lynn):

  https://www.youtube.com/watch?v=TBIOyF0N0qU

- Why Do Authors Do Pre-orders and How (Bethany Atazadeh): https://youtu.be/Q63vRihfhWY

- How to Set Up a Pre-order Campaign? (Bethany Atazadeh): https://youtu.be/h2maeknQi5Y

Chapter 6 (Make the Most of Your Cover Reveal):

- BookBrush: https://bookbrush.com/

- Blog Post by Day Leitao: Blog tours/instagram tours, what are they? Do you need one? https://dayleitao.com/blog-tours-instagram-tours-what-are-they-do-you-need-one/

- How to do a cover reveal (Bethany Atazadeh): https://youtu.be/bQ5fwCdsnuw

Chapter 8 (Sending Advanced Reader Copies):

- How to add email to receive documents on Kindle: https://www.amazon.com/gp/help/customer/display.html?nodeId=GX9XLEVV8G4DB28H

- StoryOrigin: https://storyoriginapp.com/?via=mandi

- NetGalley: https://www.netgalley.com/

- Calibre: https://calibre-ebook.com/

- Draft2Digital: https://draft2digital.com/

- Is NetGalley the Secret to More Book Reviews? Self-Published Author's Guide to NetGalley (Mandi Lynn): https://youtu.be/fhno00BZjiY

- How to Get Book Reviews on Amazon the Easy Way Using StoryOrigin (Mandi Lynn): https://youtu.be/RmZFB2Jyryc

- How to Format an eBook Using Microsoft Word & Calibre (Mandi Lynn): https://youtu.be/yU5MqK4erXc

- How to get book reviews with ARCs (Advance Review Copies) and how to do ARCs in 3 steps (Bethany Atazadeh): https://youtu.be/Aub6Ep56p78

Chapter 9 (Plan a Virtual Book Tour):

- How to Host a Virtual Book Launch (Mandi Lynn): https://youtu.be/TOtRbIvZuZQ

- How to Host a Virtual Book Signing (Bethany Atazadeh): https://youtu.be/eCpyFfmLY1w

- Blog Post by Day Leitao: Blog tours/instagram tours, what are they? Do you need one? https://dayleitao.com/blog-tours-instagram-tours-what-are-they-do-you-need-one/

Chapter 10 (Film & Edit a Book Trailer):

- *Essence* Book Trailer:
  https://youtu.be/ahmUvIaIMTU
- Original *I am Mercy* Book Trailer:
  https://youtu.be/_YCrVcGt5BI
- New *I am Mercy* Book Trailer:
  https://youtu.be/uJfotXNrFC8
- *She's Not Here* Book Trailer:
  https://youtu.be/1071b1tEPn4
- *Meet Me at the Summit* Book Trailer:
  https://www.youtube.com/watch?v=PNk8JEa
  ti3s
- How to Make a Book Trailer - The Easy Way
  (Mandi Lynn):
  https://youtu.be/2CYYp-4esQI
- Hiring a Professional to Create a Book Trailer
  (Mandi Lynn):
  https://youtu.be/ftn_cAwdSCU
- Creating a Cinematic Book Trailer (Mandi
  Lynn):
  https://youtu.be/McaKhU5PB2U
- *The Stolen Kingdom* Book Trailer (Bethany

Atazadeh):

https://youtu.be/07jihRa2QDQ

- How to Make a Book Trailer (iMovie Tutorial) Bethany Atazadeh:

  https://youtu.be/by_o10yv_IU

Chapter 11 (Release Day Marketing & Celebrations!):

- *I am Mercy* Release Day Facebook Event:

  https://www.facebook.com/events/870773016348443/?active_tab=discussion

- *The Enchanted Crown* Livestream Release Party:

  https://www.youtube.com/watch?v=GT93cQT-Wfg

- Livestream Release Party for *The Stolen Kingdom:*

  https://www.youtube.com/watch?v=8sYTHGqUDbw

- What to Do on Release Day (Bethany Atazadeh):

  https://youtu.be/m85hTvj0FUA

Chapter 12 (Sell Books at Events on Release Day & After):

- First Book Signing in Over a Year! How Many

Books Did I Sell? (Mandi Lynn):

https://www.youtube.com/watch?v=A3Tb1Fq
VApI&t=1089s

- How Many Books Can I Sell in One Day? (Mandi Lynn):

  https://www.youtube.com/watch?v=nRXwTJ
  SP4cQ&list=PLZpcZ9u8pb_oKz5yJtWIWQ
  1ml2ApLWbBg&index=2

- Signing Books at FanExpo Boston 2019 VLOG! (Mandi Lynn):

  https://www.youtube.com/watch?v=diOG8Z7
  9Xks&list=PLZpcZ9u8pb_oKz5yJtWIWQ1
  ml2ApLWbBg&index=1

- BookCon 2019 Indie Author Exhibitor Vlog! (Mandi Lynn):

  https://www.youtube.com/watch?v=R6c31qw
  FMnk&list=PLZpcZ9u8pb_oKz5yJtWIWQ1
  ml2ApLWbBg&index=3

- How to Set Up a Book Signing Event (Bethany Atazadeh):

  https://youtu.be/FzSXsZDWOKI

ABOUT THE
AUTHORS

ABOUT: MANDI

Mandi Lynn published her first novel when she was seventeen. The author of multiple books, Mandi spends her days continuing to write and creating YouTube videos to help other writers achieve their dreams of seeing their books published. Mandi is the owner of Stone Ridge Books, a company that works to help authors bring their books to life through cover design and book formatting. She is also the creator of The Book Launch Planner, a planner designed to help writers plan their book releases. You can also find Mandi designing and printing stickers through her store, Stone Ridge Stickers. When she's not creating, you can find Mandi exploring her backyard or getting lost in the woods.

BOOKS BY MANDI:

 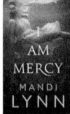  

Website: https://mandilynn.com

Instagram: @mandilynnwrites

Facebook: @mandilynnwrites

Twitter: @mandilynnwrites

YouTube: www.youtube.com/mandilynnVLOGS

Goodreads: Mandi Lynn

ABOUT: BETHANY

Bethany Atazadeh is best known for her young adult fantasy novels, The Stolen Kingdom Series, which won the Best YA Author 2020 Minnesota Author Project award. She is obsessed with stories, chocolate, and her corgi puppy, Penny.

Using her degree in English with a creative writing emphasis, Bethany enjoys helping other writers through her YouTube aka "AuthorTube" writing channel and Patreon page.

If you want to know more about when Bethany's next book will come out, visit her website below where you can sign up to receive monthly emails with exciting news, updates, and book releases.

CONNECT WITH BETHANY ON:

Website: www.bethanyatazadeh.com

Instagram: @authorbethanyatazadeh

PLAN A PROFITABLE BOOK LAUNCH

YouTube: www.youtube.com/bethanyatazadeh

Patreon: www.patreon.com/bethanyatazadeh

Goodreads: Bethany Atazadeh

BOOKS BY BETHANY: